# Motive power recognition
# LOCOMOTIVES

## 3rd Edition

# Colin J. Marsden

**LONDON**

**IAN ALLAN LTD**

First published 1981
Second Edition 1984
This Edition 1988

ISBN 0 7110 1768 9

Published by Ian Allan Ltd, Shepperton,
Surrey; and printed by Ian Allan Printing
Ltd at their works at Coombelands in
Runnymede, England

Below:
A total of 50 Class 58 purpose-built
'Railfreight' locomotives are now in
service. All are allocated to Toton depot,
and are operated by Railfreight's coal
sub-sector. On 5 November 1986
No 58015 is seen passing the site of the
former Stapleford station, with a
Bentinck-Ratcliffe CEGB working.
Colin J. Marsden

# Introduction

From the introduction during the late 1950s of large numbers of diesel and electric classes, recognition of the different types, sub-classes, their fixtures and fittings has always aroused much interest from railway observers both young and old. *Motive Power Recognition: 1 Locomotives*, has been prepared to give the reader information and illustrations of the current BR diesel, electric, electro-diesel and steam classes, in capital stock in Spring 1988.

Today recognition of the various sub-classes is far easier than in the 1960s and early 1970s due to the Total Operations Processing System (TOPS) computer numbering system, which indicates far more than just a number. The first two digits are the locomotive class, which for diesel traction is between 01-60; for dc electric or electro-diesel traction 70-79; and for ac electric locomotives 80-91. The code 97 is used for departmental locomotives, and 98 for BR-owned steam locomotives. The third digit of the number identifies the sub-class, giving information about equipment, ie if push-pull facilities are fitted, or the type of train heating. The remaining numbers represent the individual locomotive identification. For types where no sub-classifications exist, numbering commences with the third digit.

Until the mid-1980s the standard livery for locomotives was BR blue with full yellow ends, white numerals and logo. However, considerable change has occurred in this field with numerous new liveries or livery modifications being regularly reported. The main liveries operated by the sectors are, in addition to standard blue:

InterCity — two-tone grey with a waist height band of red and white.
ScotRail — similar to InterCity but with the red band replaced by blue.
Railfreight — grey body, with red base band and wrap round yellow ends, large logo and small numbers.
Railfreight Sector — In October 1987 new Railfreight Sector liveries and logos were launched and are now being progressively applied to Railfreight traction. The logos are shown on page 160.
Network SouthEast — blue and grey body with red and white waist height band.

In addition to the standard sector liveries a number of 'one-offs' exist, which are detailed in the text where possible.

Since publication of the last edition of *Motive Power Recognition: 1 Locomotives*, Classes 13, 25, 27, 46 and 82 have been completely eliminated, while considerable changes have taken place to other classes, with major refurbishing of some types. New BR classes introduced since the previous edition have been 89, 90 and 91 on the electric front, and the Class 59 privately-owned diesels — the first privately owned main line locomotive type on BR.

For the first time it has been possible to include cab illustrations of most classes, which have been numbered for easy identification of all components. **It must be emphasised that members of the public are not permitted to enter cabs.**

The technical text at the start of each section has been fully revised to take account of recent changes, and now includes details of former classifications and the new sector ownership, while main detail differences have been listed for each class. For most classes a number of illustrations have been numerically detailed to show the positions of major components, and it is hoped that this, in conjunction with the line drawings, will assist readers in the fuller understanding of the complex motive power subject.

I would like to take this opportunity to thank everybody who has assisted with illustrations and technical information for inclusion in this project, especially to Michael Collins, John Tuffs and Tom Noble who have gone out of their way to assist, often making special photographic trips, and Graham Fenn for supplying drawings.

The Editor of this volume would like to be notified of any major detail differences that have been omitted from this book by sending them, together with an illustration if possible, to: The Editor, Motive Power Recognition, Ian Allan Ltd, Coombelands House, Coombelands Lane, Addlestone, Weybridge, Surrey KT15 1HY.

*Colin J. Marsden*
*Dawlish*
*March 1988*

# Locomotive Types and Classifications

| Class | Number range | Type | Detail differences | Regions of allocation |
|---|---|---|---|---|
| 03 | 03073-03170 | 0-6-0 | | Midland |
| 08/0 | 08011-08954 | 0-6-0 | Standard locomotive | All Regions |
| 08/9 | 08993-08995 | 0-6-0 | Cut-down cab 08/0 | Western |
| 09 | 09001-09026 | 0-6-0 | | Southern |
| 20 | 20001-20228 | Bo-Bo | | Midland, Eastern, Scottish |
| 26/0 | 26001-26015 | Bo-Bo | Basic locomotive — freight | Scottish |
| 26/1 | 26021-26046 | Bo-Bo | Modified equipment | Scottish |
| 31/1 | 31101-31327 | A1A-A1A | Basic locomotive | Midland, Eastern, Western |
| 31/4 | 31401-31469 | A1A-A1A | Fitted with electric/dual train heat equipment | Midland, Eastern, Western |
| 33/0 | 33002-33065 | Bo-Bo | Basic locomotive | Southern |
| 33/1 | 33101-33119 | Bo-Bo | Fitted with push-pull equipment | Southern |
| 33/2 | 33201-33212 | Bo-Bo | Narrow-bodied locomotives | Southern |
| 37/0 | 37001-37326 | Co-Co | Basic locomotive | Eastern, Western, Scottish |
| 37/3 | 37350-37381 | Co-Co | Fitted with CP7 bogies | Eastern, Western |
| 37/4 | 37401-37431 | Co-Co | Fitted with ETS | Western, Scottish |
| 37/5 | 37501-37699 | Co-Co | Refurbished with RA5 | Eastern, Western |
| 37/7 | 37701-37899 | Co-Co | Refurbished with RA7 | Eastern, Western |
| 37/9 | 37901-37906 | Co-Co | Fitted with experimental engines | Western |
| 43 | 43002-43198 | Bo-Bo | IC125 Power Cars | Eastern, Western, Scottish |
| 45/0 | 45007-45070 | 1Co-Co1 | No train heat | Eastern |
| 45/1 | 45103-45150 | 1Co-Co1 | Fitted with ETS | Eastern |
| 47/0 | 47002-47299 | Co-Co | Basic locomotive | Eastern, Midland, Western, Scottish |
| 47/3 | 47301-47381 | Co-Co | Built without facilities for train heat | Eastern, Midland, Western |
| 47/4 | 47401-47665 | Co-Co | Fitted with electric/dual heat equipment | Eastern, Midland, Western, Scottish |
| 47/7 | 47701-47716 | Co-Co | Fitted for RCH push-pull operation | Scottish |
| 47/9 | 47901 | Co-Co | Fitted with experimental engine | Western |
| 50/0 | 50001-50050 | Co-Co | | Western |
| 50/1 | 50149 | Co-Co | Railfreight Class 50 | Western |
| 56 | 56001-56135 | Co-Co | | Midland, Western |
| 58 | 58001-58050 | Co-Co | | Midland |
| 59 | 59001-59004 | Co-Co | Privately owned freight locomotive | Foster Yeoman Ltd |

4

| | | | | |
|---|---|---|---|---|
| 73/0 | 73001-73006 | Bo-Bo | Prototype design | Southern |
| 73/1 | 73101-73142 | Bo-Bo | Production design | Southern |
| 73/2 | 73201-73212 | Bo-Bo | Gatwick Express dedicated | Southern |
| 81 | 81002-81022 | Bo-Bo | | Scottish |
| 83 | 83009-83012 | Bo-Bo | | Midland |
| 85 | 85002-85040 | Bo-Bo | | Midland |
| 86/1 | 86101-86103 | Bo-Bo | Fitted with Class 87 equipment | Midland |
| 86/2 | 86204-86261 | Bo-Bo | Standard locomotive | Midland |
| 86/4 | 86401-86439 | Bo-Bo | Modified, and MU fitted | Midland |
| 87/0 | 87001-87035 | Bo-Bo | Basic locomotive | Midland |
| 87/1 | 87101 | Bo-Bo | Test locomotive, fitted with thyristor control equipment | Midland |
| 89 | 89001 | Co-Co | Evaluation locomotive | |
| 90 | 90001-90050* | Bo-Bo | | Midland |
| 91 | 91001-91031* | Bo-Bo | New generation electric locomotive | Eastern |
| 98 | 7, 8, 9 | 2-6-2T | Vale of Rheidol steam locomotives | Midland |
| 98 | 10 | 0-6-0 | Vale of Rheidol diesel | Midland |

*Still being introduced

## Sector Ownership Codes

All locomotives are allocated to a specific operating sector — for individual allocations reference should be made to Ian Allan abc BR Locomotives and Motive Power Monthly magazine, August 1988. Letters are given at the bottom of each technical description to indicate the owning sector viz:

D   Departmental
F   Railfreight
I   InterCity
L   Freightliner
N   Network SouthEast
P   Provincial
R   Parcels

# Class 03

| | |
|---|---|
| **Former Class codes:** | DJ15, later D2/2, 2/1 |
| **Present number range:** | 03073-03170 |
| **Former number range:** | D2000-D2199/D2370-D2399 |
| **Original number range:** | 11187-11211* |
| **Built by:** | BR Swindon and Doncaster |
| **Introduced:** | 1957-61 |
| **Wheel arrangement:** | 0-6-0 |
| **Weight (operational):** | 30.3 tonnes |
| **Height:** | 11ft 9⅜in (3.59m) |
| **Width:** | 8ft 6in (2.59m) |
| **Length:** | 26ft 0in (7.92m) |
| **Minimum curve negotiable:** | 2 chains (40.23m) |
| **Maximum speed:** | 28½mph (42km/h) |
| **Wheelbase:** | 9ft 0in (2.74m) |
| **Wheel diameter:** | 3ft 7in (1.09m) |
| **Brake type:** | Dual |
| **Sanding equipment:** | Pneumatic |
| **Route availability:** | 1 |
| **Multiple coupling restriction:** | Not multiple fitted |
| **Brake force:** | 13 tonnes |
| **Engine type:** | Gardner 8L3 |
| **Engine horsepower:** | 204hp (152kW) |
| **Power at rail:** | 152hp (113kW) |
| **Tractive effort:** | 15,300lb (68kN) |
| **Cylinder bore:** | 5½in (0.13m) |
| **Cylinder stroke:** | 7¾in (0.19m) |
| **Transmission (engine-gearbox):** | Fluidrive Type 23 HYD |
| **Transmission (gearbox):** | Wilson-Drewry CA5 R7 |
| **Transmission (final drive):** | SCG Type RF11 |
| **Gear ratio:** | 1st 4.07 : 1, 2nd 2.33 : 1, 3rd 1.55 : 1, 4th 1 : 1, 5th 1 : 1.87 |
| **Fuel tank capacity:** | 300gal (1,364lit) |
| **Cooling water capacity:** | 40gal (182lit) |
| **Lubricating oil capacity:** | 8gal (36lit) |
| **Regions of allocation:** | Midland |
| **Sector ownership:** | D, F |

This class is scheduled for early withdrawal.

* The original numbers allocated to this class were not carried.

Below:
*This drawing represents a dual braked example, fitted with buffer beam air connections only.*

Above:
*Class 03 cab layout. 1. Master switch on/off, 2. Cab socket fuse, 3. Oil pressure fuse, 4. Front light fuse, 5. Rear light fuse, 6. Heater fuse, 7. Wiper fuse, 8. Oil pressure warning lamp, 9. Ampmeter, 10. Water temperature gauge, 11. Oil pressure warning lamp, 12. Front light switches (× 2), 13. Panel light switch, 14. Cab heat switches, 15. Cab light switch, 16. Rear light switches (× 2), 17. Gearbox air pressure, 18. Vacuum brake gauge, 19. Duplex pressure gauge, 20. Brake pipe pressure gauge, 21. Lub oil pressure gauge, 22. Rev counter, 23. Speedometer, 24. Fuel gauge, 25. Sanding lever, 26. Forward/reverse lever, 27. Throttle, 28. Loco brake valve, 29. Horn valve, 30. Gear selector, 31. Train brake valve. Cab illustration of No 03059.   Michael J. Collins*

Below:
*The once 230-strong fleet of Class 03 0-6-0 diesel mechanical shunting locomotives now consists of just three members, all of which sport dual brake equipment, identifiable by both vacuum and air connections being present on the buffer beams. No 03059 is illustrated.   Michael J. Collins*

Above:
*The standard livery for the Class 03 fleet is blue with yellow and black 'wasp' warning ends, some detail variation does exist to colours of buffer beams. No 03059 is again illustrated — this time from the cab or rear end.*   Colin J. Marsden

Below:
*Class 03 in detail. 1. Exhaust stack (Saxa style), 2. Front indicator lights, 3. Main reservoir pipe, 4. Air brake pipe, 5. Vacuum pipe, 6. Screw coupling, 7. Warning horns, 8. Air brake reservoir. Locomotive No 03371 is illustrated, which is typical of a later built locomotive having the 'Saxa' style exhaust stack, earlier locomotives having the 'Flower Pot' type, as illustrated in the previous plate.*   John Tuffs

Below:
*In early 1987 Birkenhead's No 03162 was repainted into BR green livery, and given its original number D2162. The repainting was carried out to commemorate the 106 years of Birkenhead South depot.*   A. C.Smallbone

Bottom:
*Over the years a number of problems have been encountered with Class 03s failing to operate track circuit equipment correctly. This problem has been overcome by the attachment of a match truck (TOPS code ZS) to one end, which remains semi-permanently coupled to the locomotive. Internal maintenance on the Class 03s is effected via the side doors and removable roof sections. Dual brake-fitted No 03371 stands coupled to vacuum-only match wagon No DB705370 at Bradford in 1983.*
Colin J. Marsden

# Class 08

| | |
|---|---|
| **Former Class codes:** | DEJ4, later D3/2, 3/1 |
| **Present number range (08/0):** | 08011-08954 |
| **(08/9):** | 08993-08995 |
| **Former number range:** | D3000-D4192 |
| **Original number range:** | 13000-13366 |
| **Built by:** | BR Crewe, Derby, Doncaster, Darlington and Horwich |
| **Introduced:** | 1953-59 |
| **Wheel arrangement:** | 0-6-0 |
| **Weight (operational):** | 48-49 tonnes |
| **Height (08/0):** | 12ft 8⅝in (3.87m) |
| **(08/9):** | 11ft 10in (3.60m) |
| **Width:** | 8ft 6in (2.59m) |
| **Length:** | 29ft 3in (8.91m) |
| **Minimum curve negotiable:** | 3 chains (60.35m) |
| **Maximum speed:** | 15-20mph (25-33km/h) |
| **Wheelbase:** | 11ft 6in (3.50m) |
| **Wheel diameter:** | 4ft 6in (1.37m) |
| **Brake type:** | Vacuum, air or dual |
| **Sanding equipment:** | Pneumatic |
| **Route availability:** | 5 |
| **Multiple coupling restriction:** | Not multiple fitted |
| **Brake force:** | 19 tonnes |
| **Engine type:** | English Electric 6K |
| **Engine horsepower:** | 350hp (261kW) |
| **Power at rail:** | 194hp (260kW) |
| **Tractive effort:** | 35,000lb (156kN) |
| **Cylinder bore:** | 10in (0.25m) |
| **Cylinder stroke:** | 12in (0.30m) |
| **Main generator type:** | EE801-8E |
| **Auxiliary generator type:** | EE736-2D |
| **Number of traction motors:** | 2 |
| **Traction motor type:** | EE506-6A or EE506-7C |
| **Gear ratio:** | 23.9 : 1 |
| **Fuel tank capacity:** | 668gal (3,037lit) |
| **Cooling water capacity:** | 140gal (636lit) |
| **Lubricating oil capacity:** | 45gal (204lit) |
| **Regions of allocation:** | Eastern, Midland, Western, Scottish, Southern |
| **Sector ownership:** | D, F, I, L, P, R |

## Subclass variations

Class 08/0: Standard locomotive, standard BR shunting power, direct descendant of pre-nationalisation types.
Class 08/9: reduced cab height locomotive, used on BPGV lines.

Below:
*This drawing is representative of a vacuum braked only example. For various details please see illustrations.*

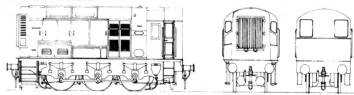

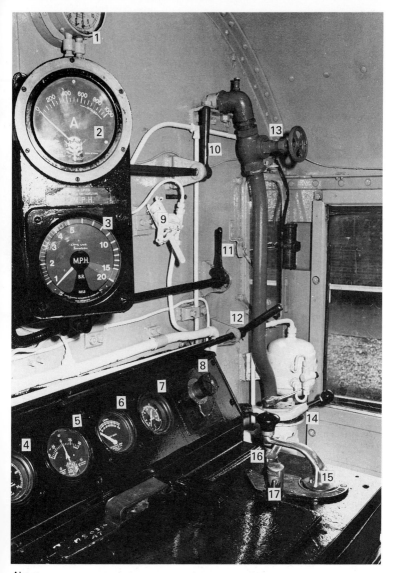

Above:
*Class 08 cab layout (unrefurbished), also applicable to Class 09. 1. Vacuum brake gauge, 2. Ampmeter, 3. Speedometer, 4. Brake cylinder pressure gauge, 5. Battery charge/ discharge indicator, 6. Duplex pressure gauge, 7. Water temperature gauge, 8. Inspection light socket, 9. Brake release trigger, 10. Emergency brake valve, 11. Sanding valve, 12. Locomotive brake valve, 13. Cab heat control, 14. Train brake valve, 15. Power controller, 16. Master switch, 17. Key socket.* Colin J. Marsden

Above:
*The standard BR shunting locomotive in use today is the Class 08, of which over 500 are still in service classified as 08/0. There are a number of detail differences, but the standard locomotive is a vacuum braked machine, as depicted by this illustration of No 08273 shown from the nose or front end.* Colin J. Marsden

Below:
*Although all Class 08 locomotives were built with only vacuum brake equipment, the larger proportion of the fleet now have dual brakes; identification of the brake type is achieved by reference to the hoses on the buffer beam. This illustration of No 08880 shows the locomotive from the back or cab end, and reference to the buffer beam will show this to be a dual-braked example.* Colin J. Marsden

Above:
*Like the Class 03s, some Class 08s have high level or waist height duplicate air pipes, as displayed on this front end illustration. This front end is also applicable for Class 09. 1. Main reservoir pipe, 2. Brake pipe, 3. High level main reservoir pipe, 4. High level brake pipe, 5. High level dual cock, 6. Vacuum pipe, 7. Coupling, 8. Front marker light (×3), 9. Radiator filler point, 10. Radiator level sight glass.* Colin J. Marsden

Below:
*Class 08 side and rear end layout. 1. Removable roof sections, 2. Removable side access doors, 3. Vacuum exhauster box, 4. Battery box, 5. Battery isolating switch box, 6. Air compressor box, 7. Marker lights, 8. Vacuum pipe, 9. Main reservoir pipe, 10. Brake pipe, 11. Coupling, 12. Fuel entry point, 13. Sand box. Locomotive No 08904 is illustrated.* Colin J. Marsden

Above:
*The standard Class 08/0 fitted with either vacuum or dual brake equipment can be found working on all regions. As a rule those fitted with high level pipes are found on the SR where they can operate with SR EMU/DMU stock. Painted in standard blue livery, No 08929 is seen at Eastleigh attached to the depot's M&EE crane.* Colin J. Marsden

Below:
*With the rapid reduction in vacuum braked stock and the ever increasing number of air braked vehicles in service, a number of Class 08s were fitted with air brakes only in the late 1970s and early 1980s. Locomotives so modified can be identified by the omission of a vacuum pipe on the buffer beam. One such example, No 08463 is seen shunting at BREL Derby Locomotive Works in 1986.* Colin J. Marsden

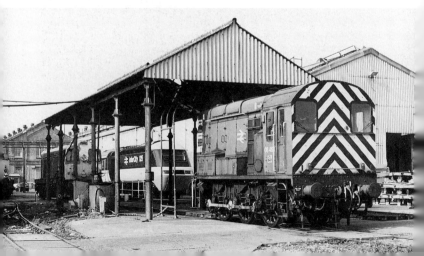

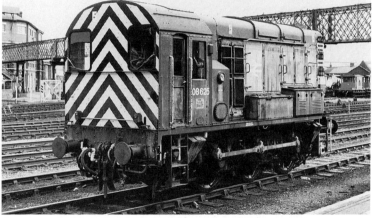

Top:
*To enable IC125, and other stock fitted with solid-shank buck-eye couplers to be attached to Class 08s, a fleet of 14 locomotives are fitted with drop-head buck-eye couplers. These locomotives are allocated to strategic depots where coaching stock or IC125 movements are required. Old Oak Common-allocated No 08480 is illustrated with the buck-eye in the lowered position.* Colin J. Marsden

Above:
*When constructed, the Class 08s were fitted with four marker lights on both the front and rear ends. However, over the years the central lights at both top and bottom have been removed on many examples, as displayed in this illustration of No 08625 at Derby.* Colin J. Marsden

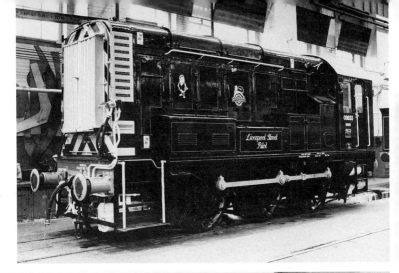

Top:
*Some official naming of Class 08s has been carried out in recent years. This has included such names as* Liverpool Street Pilot, The Doncaster Postman, *and the three Class 08/9 locomotives. As well as naming, some revision to liveries has been permitted with locomotives emerging in most 'Sector' colours as well as a number of former Railway Company schemes. No 08833, painted in Great Eastern blue and named* Liverpool Street Pilot, *is illustrated at its home depot of Stratford.* Brian Morrison

Above:
*Carrying its original number and livery, No D3018 (now 08011) was restored to its original condition in 1985 by Bletchley depot and is seen displayed at BREL Wolverton Works Open Day. After the event the locomotive was returned to traffic in green livery, but carrying its TOPS number.* Colin J. Marsden

Above:
*The first Class 08, No 08834, to emerge in Railfreight Sector colours was released from Stratford Major depot in October 1987 and looked very smart carrying the Railfreight Speedlink livery. Note the cast BR logo and Stratford Sparrow crest on the battery box.*
Colin J. Marsden

Below:
*In 1985 the Class 08/9 sub-class was introduced to cater for locomotives with reduced cab height for the BPGV line. Three locomotives are currently in service, Nos 08993-08995. Now withdrawn, No 08991 and No 08993 are illustrated.*   S. K. Miles

# Class 09

| | |
|---|---|
| **Former Class codes:** | DEJ4, later 3/1 |
| **Number range:** | 09001-09026 |
| **Former number range:** | D3665-71, D3719-21, D4099-114 |
| **Built by:** | BR Darlington, Horwich |
| **Introduced:** | 1959-62 |
| **Wheel arrangement:** | 0-6-0 |
| **Weight (operational):** | 49 tonnes |
| **Height:** | 12ft 8⅝in (3.87m) |
| **Width:** | 8ft 6in (2.59m) |
| **Length:** | 29ft 3in (8.91m) |
| **Minimum curve negotiable:** | 3 chains (60.35m) |
| **Maximum speed:** | 27mph (34km/h) |
| **Wheelbase:** | 11ft 6in (3.50m) |
| **Wheel diameter:** | 4ft 6in (1.37m) |
| **Brake type:** | Dual |
| **Sanding equipment:** | Pneumatic |
| **Route availability:** | 5 |
| **Multiple coupling restriction:** | Not multiple fitted |
| **Brake force:** | 19 tonnes |
| **Engine type:** | English Electric 6K |
| **Horsepower:** | 350hp (261kW) |
| **Power at rail:** | 194hp (260kW) |
| **Tractive effort:** | 35,000lb (156kN) |
| **Cylinder bore:** | 10in (0.25m) |
| **Cylinder stroke:** | 12in (0.30m) |
| **Main generator type:** | EE801-8E |
| **Auxiliary generator type:** | EE736-2D |
| **Number of traction motors:** | 2 |
| **Traction motor type:** | EE506-6A or EE506-7C |
| **Gear ratio:** | 23.9 : 1 |
| **Fuel tank capacity:** | 668gal (3,037lit) |
| **Cooling water capacity:** | 140gal (636lit) |
| **Lubricating oil capacity:** | 45gal (204lit) |
| **Region of allocation:** | Southern |
| **Sector ownership:** | D, F, I, N |

Higher speed variant of Class 08.    One example of this class, No 09017, is now in departmental stock as No 97806 at Cardiff.

Below:
*This drawing is representative of the majority of the fleet; all locomotives are fitted with dual brake equipment and high level extension pipes. Differences may occur in end fittings. This drawing has been prepared to the original condition of the locomotive, with a ladder on the nose end by the side of the radiator.*

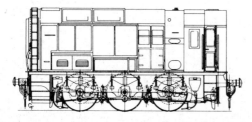
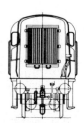

Above:
*As will be seen if this illustration of a Class 09 and the previous illustrations of Class 08s are compared, there are virtually no visual differences between these two classes, the main operational difference being speed, which is higher on the Class 09. All Class 09s are fitted with dual brake equipment, and, except for one which is in departmental service, are allocated to the SR. No 09025 is illustrated.* Colin J. Marsden

Below:
*Class 09 in detail: 1. Warning horn, 2. Fuel tank gauge, 3. Air intakes, 4. Battery isolating switch, 5. Battery box, 6. Vacuum exhauster, 7. Air compressor, 8. Connecting rod, 9. Sand boxes, 10. Removable side inspection doors.* Colin J. Marsden

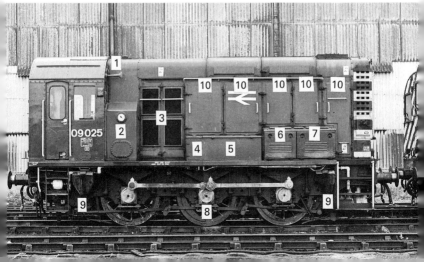

# Class 20

| | |
|---|---|
| **Former Class codes:** | D10/3, later 10/3 |
| **Number range:** | 20001-20199, 20200-20228 |
| **Former number range:** | D8000-D8199, D8300-D8327 |
| **Built by:** | EE & RSH Ltd |
| **Introduced:** | 1957-68 |
| **Wheel arrangement:** | Bo-Bo |
| **Weight (operational):** | 73 tonnes |
| **Height:** | 12ft 7⅝in (3.84m) |
| **Width:** | 8ft 9in (2.66m) |
| **Length:** | 46ft 9¼in (14.26m) |
| **Minimum curve negotiable:** | 3½ chains (70.40m) |
| **Maximum speed:** | 60mph (97km/h)* |
| **Wheelbase:** | 32ft 6in (9.90m) |
| **Bogie wheelbase:** | 8ft 6in (2.59m) |
| **Bogie pivot centres:** | 24ft 0in (7.31m) |
| **Wheel diameter:** | 3ft 7in (1.09m) |
| **Brake type:** | Dual |
| **Sanding equipment:** | Pneumatic |
| **Route availability:** | 5 |
| **Multiple coupling restriction:** | Blue Star |
| **Brake force:** | 35 tonnes |
| **Engine type:** | English Electric 8SVT Mk 11 |
| **Engine horsepower:** | 1,000hp (745kW) |
| **Power at rail:** | 770hp (574kW) |
| **Tractive effort:** | 42,000lb (187kN) |
| **Cylinder bore:** | 10in (0.25m) |
| **Cylinder stroke:** | 12in (0.30m) |
| **Main generator type:** | EE819-3C |
| **Auxiliary generator type:** | EE911-2B |
| **Number of traction motors:** | 4 |
| **Traction motor type (20001-049):** | EE526-5D |
| **(20051-228):** | EE526-8D |
| **Gear ratio:** | 63 : 17 |
| **Fuel tank capacity:** | 380gal (1,727lit)† |
| **Cooling water capacity:** | 130gal (591lit) |
| **Lubricating oil capacity:** | 100gal (455lit) |
| **Regions of allocation:** | Midland, Eastern, Scottish |
| **Sector ownership:** | D, F |

Remote control radio equipment is installed on Nos 20058/087.
Transponder coding equipment is installed on Nos 20004/06/16/20/26/41/49/52/53/65/72/
73/80/81/82/99/101/105/113.
Snowplough brackets fitted on Nos 20028-34/70-127/29-88/90-228.
Slow speed control equipment fitted to 20004-8/10/13/19/20/21/23/26/28/32/34/40/41/47/
51/52/55-60/65/70-73/75/78/80/81/82/84/85/87/90/94/99/101/103-106/108/113/117/120/128/
129/130/132-135/140-143/147/157-160/163/166/168/169/170/172/173/177-179/182/183/186-
190/192-196/198/199/201-209/211-215/218/222/224-227.
* The maximum speed of the Class 20s was 75mph (121km/h) until May 1987.
† No 20084 is fitted with additional fuel tanks, giving a fuel capacity of 1,040gal
(4,728lit).

## Main body variations

Nos 20001-128 were built with disc-type train reporting equipment, while Nos 20129-228
were built with 4-position headcode boxes.
    As refurbishment takes place, marker lights are being installed in place of discs and
headcode boxes.

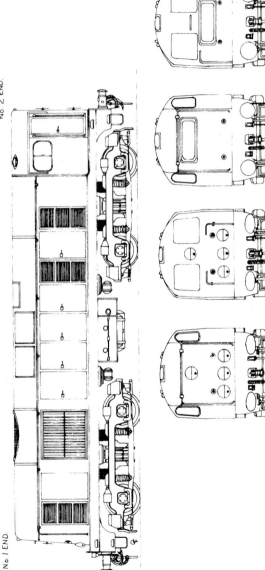

Above:
This side elevation is representative of locomotives Nos 20001-20128 fitted with the disc train identification system. Four nose/rear ends are shown, the disc ends are carried on locomotives Nos 20001-128 and the four position route indicator style ends on Nos 20129-228. It will be noted that different style buffers are shown, although it is not constant that disc headcoded examples carry oval buffers and headcode box members the round style. One locomotive has been observed in traffic with round buffers on one end and oval at the other!

Below:
*The first 128 Class 20s (Nos 20001-128) were built with the disc train identification system, whereas the remaining 100 (20129-228) were fitted with the four-character identification system. The Class 20 fleet are unique amongst today's main line BR traction as they have a cab at only one end; this can cause problems with vision of the track ahead being impaired, and often two locomotives are coupled nose to nose. The above illustration shows No 20061, an example of the original batch, whilst the lower plate shows No 20161, a machine built with four-character box.* Both: Colin J. Marsden

Above:
*Class 20 cab layout: 1. Locomotive brake valve, 2. Train brake valve, 3. Two-tone warning horn valve, 4. Engine stopped warning light, 5. Wheelslip warning light, 6. General fault warning light, 7. Start button, 8. Stop button, 9. Anti-slip brake button, 10. AWS reset button, 11. Vacuum gauge, 12. Speedometer, 13. Air brake pipe gauge, 14. Bogie brake cylinder gauge, 15. Ampmeter, 16. Main reservoir pressure gauge, 17. Slow speed speedometer, 18. Master switch (FOR/EO/REV/OFF), 19. Power controller, 20. AWS indicator, 21. Slow speed control switch gear, 22. Fire alarm test button. Cab illustrated from locomotive No 20008.   Colin J. Marsden*

Below:
*From the mid-1980s a major programme of Class 20 refurbishment commenced, which should take at least some of the class into the next century. Apart from major internal rebuilding, the work included the removal of the former headcode discs, and the installation of sealed beam lights. Refurbished No 20163 painted in 'Railfreight' livery is illustrated.   Colin J. Marsden*

Above:
*Class 20 end layout — equipment applicable to both ends. 1. Horns (behind grille), 2. Marker discs (lights behind), 3. Engine control air pipe, 4. Main reservoir pipe, 5. Vacuum pipe, 6. Coupling, 7. Multiple control jumper receptacle, 8. Multiple control jumper cable, 9. Brake pipe.* Colin J. Marsden

Above:
*Cab end view of disc headcode Class 20, with five identification discs each with a lamp behind; above the two outer discs at the bottom are red 'tail' indicators. Two different buffer designs can be found on the Class 20 fleet. When built, the original locomotives had oval buffers, and the later examples round ones, but today there is no hard-and-fast rule. Locomotive No 20017 is illustrated.*   Colin J. Marsden

Below:
*Locomotives Nos 20129-228 which are fitted with the four-character headcode system, have a much cleaner looking body end than those fitted with discs, but of course still retain the red 'tail' marker lights. Round buffer-fitted No 20135 is illustrated.*
Colin J. Marsden

Above:
*The ends of refurbished disc headcoded examples look something of a mess, as the discs have been removed but all four indicator lights have been left in situ. This, together with the 'tail' indicators, gives no fewer than six end lights. Sporting Railfreight livery No 20090 is shown at BREL Derby Works.   Colin J. Marsden*

Below:
*A high proportion of the Class 20 fleet are fitted with snowplough brackets, however only a handful actually carry the three-piece miniature ploughs at any one time. No 20143 illustrates the snowplough fitting. The six hinged bodyside doors give access to all technical equipment, but if large items need removal the roof sections are lifted off.   Colin J. Marsden*

Below:
*The two body sides of the Class 20 are virtually identical, except for an additional door at the cab end in place of a louvred panel on one side. If this and the previous illustration are compared this is clearly seen. No 20008, which is illustrated, also shows a revised front layout, with the two redundant marker lights removed.* Colin J. Marsden

Bottom:
*The Class 20 fleet are painted in either BR standard blue, or the Railfreight grey livery. Over the coming years the majority of the fleet should be repainted into Railfreight colours, as all but 44 are owned by that sector. The remaining locomotives operate under the departmental flag and should therefore remain in standard blue. Railfreight No 20163 is illustrated.* Colin J. Marsden

Above:
Class 20 in detail. A. No 1 end, B. No 2 end, 1. Traction motor cooling fan and air compressor compartment, 2. Vacuum exhauster compartment, 3. Radiator unit, 4. Radiator fan, 5. Lubricating and fuel pump, 6. Engine compartment, 7. Generator compartment, 8. Traction motor blower compartment, 9. Electric control cubicle, 10. Driver's cab area, 11. Sandboxes, 12. Mileage counter, 13. Primary suspension, 14. Secondary suspension, 15. Brake cylinder, 16. Battery box, with air reservoirs behind, 17. Fire bottle pull handle, 18. Fuel tank gauge. Colin J. Marsden

Below:
In early 1987, Tinsley depot repainted Nos 20030 and 20064 into green livery, with a grey roof, red solebar, and black window surround. Whilst the livery looks very smart, the adoption of a red solebar and black window surround does spoil the overall effect. Nos 20064/030, plus Railfreight-liveried No 20118 pass Gatwick Airport in May 1987 with a Railtour from Brighton to Sheffield. Colin J. Marsden

# Class 26

| | |
|---|---|
| **Former Class codes (D5300-19):** | D11/4, later 11/6 |
| **(D5320-46):** | 11/6A |
| **Present number range (26/0):** | 26001-26015 |
| **(26/1):** | 26021-26046 |
| **Former number range:** | D5300-D5346 |
| **Built by:** | Birmingham RC&W Ltd |
| **Introduced:** | 1958-59 |
| **Wheel arrangement:** | Bo-Bo |
| **Weight (operational):** | 75-79 tonnes |
| **Height:** | 12ft 8in (3.86m) |
| **Width:** | 8ft 10in (2.69m) |
| **Length:** | 50ft 9in (15.47m) |
| **Minimum curve negotiable:** | 5 chains (100.58m) |
| **Maximum speed:** | 75mph (121km/h) |
| **Wheelbase:** | 39ft 0in (11.88m) |
| **Bogie wheelbase:** | 10ft 0in (3.04m) |
| **Bogie pivot centres:** | 29ft 0in (8.83m) |
| **Wheel diameter:** | 3ft 7in (1.09m) |
| **Brake type:** | Dual |
| **Sanding equipment:** | Pneumatic |
| **Route availability:** | 6 |
| **Heating type:** | Not fitted |
| **Multiple coupling restriction:** | Blue Star |
| **Brake force:** | 35 tonnes |
| **Engine type:** | Sulzer 6LDA28B |
| **Engine horsepower:** | 1,160hp (864kW) |
| **Power at rail:** | 900hp (671kW) |
| **Tractive effort:** | 42,000lb (187kN) |
| **Cylinder bore:** | 11in (0.27m) |
| **Cylinder stroke:** | 14in (0.35m) |
| **Main generator type:** | CG391-A1 |
| **Auxiliary generator type:** | CAG193-1A |
| **Number of traction motors:** | 4 |
| **Traction motor type (26/0):** | CP171-A1 |
| **(26/1):** | CP171-D3 |
| **Gear ratio:** | 63 : 16 |
| **Fuel tank capacity:** | 500gal (2,273lit) |
| **Cooling water capacity:** | 190gal (864lit) |
| **Lubricating oil capacity:** | 100gal (455lit) |
| **Region of allocation:** | Scottish |
| **Sector ownership:** | D, F |

## Subclass variations

Two sub-classes exist within Class 26. All locomotives have been refurbished.

Class 26/0: 26001-015, within this sub-class two distinct groups exist 26001-07, which weigh 75 tonnes, and are fitted with slow speed control equipment, and 26008-15 which are the standard locomotive, and weigh 79 tonnes. All 26/0s were originally fitted with leaf secondary springing, but following refurbishment most now have coil springing and modified bogies. On Class 26/0 locomotives the multiple control jumper cable has its housing on the buffer beam.

Class 26/1: 26021-046, this sub-class weigh 79 tonnes, and are fitted with later design traction motors. 26/1 locomotives have their multiple control jumper cable housed on the locomotive body front (driver's side).

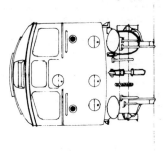

Above:
Two different Class 26 designs are currently in traffic; this drawing is representative of locomotives Nos 26.008-019, fitted with leaf secondary springing, oval buffers, steam heating and multiple-unit equipment mounted on the buffer beam.

Above:

*Class 26/1 cab layout. 1. Train brake valve, 2. Locomotive brake valve, 3. AWS reset button, 4. Start switch, 5. Master switch, 6. Power controller, 7. Engine stop button, 8. Horn valve, 9. Brake pipe gauge, 10. Vacuum gauge, 11. Brake cylinder gauge, 12. Speedometer, 13. Ampmeter, 14. Windscreen wiper control, 15. Indicator dimmer switch, 16. Engine stopped light, 17. Wheel slip light, 18. Fault light, 19. Cab heat switch, 20. Main reservoir gauge, 21. Brake release cock, 22. Desk light switch, 23. Demister switch, 24. AWS indicator, 25. Brake selection panel.* Tom Noble

Below left:

*Class 26 front end layout. The ends of the two sub-classes do differ, with the position of the multiple control jumper being housed on the buffer beam on Class 26/0, and on the bodywork on Class 26/1. Class 26/1 front end, equipment in similar position on 26/0. 1. Red 'tail' marker lights, 2. Marker lights, 3. Main reservoir pipe, 4. Engine control air pipe, 5. Brake pipe, 6. Vacuum pipe, 7. Multiple control jumper socket, 8. Multiple control jumper cable, 9. Coupling.* Tom Noble

Below:
*Two sub-classes exist within the Class 26 fleet — 26/0, and 26/1 — and some detail differences exist between the two types, and within the sub-classes themselves. The view (below) shows a Class 26/0 from its No 2 end, while (bottom) shows a Class 26/1 from its No 1 end. Main items of equipment are marked. 1. Fuel tank, 2. Battery box, 3. Air brake equipment, 4. Boiler (removed), and compressor compartment, 5. Power unit and generator compartment, 6. Traction motor blower compartment, 7. Radiator compartment, 8. Engine room side door, 9. Bogie axleboxes.  Both: Tom Noble*

Left:
*When introduced, the first 20 locomotives (now Class 26/0) were fitted with oval buffers, the remainder having the round variety. However, following refurbishing a number of alterations have been reported. This illustration shows the front end layout of a Class 26/0. Note the position of the multiple control jumper cable on the buffer beam.*
Tom Noble

# Class 31

| Sub-Class: | 31/1 | 31/4 |
|---|---|---|
| Former Class codes: | D14/2, later 14/2 | — |
| Number range: | 31101-31327 | 31401-31469 |
| Former number range: | D5518-D5862 | From main fleet |
| Built by: | Brush Ltd | Brush Ltd |
| Introduced: | 1958-62 | As 31/4 1972-87 |
| Wheel arrangement: | A1A-A1A | A1A-A1A |
| Weight (operational): | 108-110 tonnes | 110-113 tonnes |
| Height: | 12ft 7in (3.83m) | 12ft 7in (3.83m) |
| Width: | 8ft 9in (2.66m) | 8ft 9in (2.66m) |
| Length: | 56ft 9in (17.29m) | 56ft 9in (17.29m) |
| Minimum curve negotiable: | 4½ chains (90.52m) | 4½ chains (90.52m) |
| Maximum speed (31101-31116): | 80mph (129km/h) | 90mph (145km/h) |
| (31117-31327): | 90mph (145km/h) | — |
| Wheelbase: | 42ft 10in (13.05m) | 42ft 10in (13.05m) |
| Bogie wheelbase: | 14ft 0in (4.26m) | 14ft 0in (4.26m) |
| Bogie pivot centres: | 28ft 10in (8.78m) | 28ft 10in (8.78m) |
| Wheel diameter (driving): | 3ft 7in (1.09m) | 3ft 7in (1.09m) |
| (unpowered): | 3ft 3½in (1.00m) | 3ft 3½in (1.00m) |
| Brake type: | Dual | Dual |
| Sanding equipment: | Pneumatic | Pneumatic |
| Route availability: | 5 | 6 |
| Heating type (if fitted): | Steam — Spanner Mk 1* | Electric or dual — Index 66* |
| Multiple coupling restriction: | Blue Star | Blue Star |
| Brake force: | 49 tonnes | 49 tonnes |
| Engine type: | EE 12SVT | EE 12SVT |
| Engine horsepower: | 1,470hp (1,097kW) | 1,470hp (1,097kW) |
| Power at rail: | 1,170hp (872kW) | 1,170hp (872kW) |
| Tractive effort (31101-31116): | 42,800lb (190kN) | 39,500lb (160kN) |
| (31117-31327): | 39,500lb (160kN) | — |
| Cylinder bore: | 10in (0.25m) | 10in (0.25m) |
| Cylinder stroke: | 12in (0.30m) | 12in (0.30m) |
| Main generator type: | Brush TG160-48 | Brush TG160-48 |
| Auxiliary generator type: | Brush TG69-42 | Brush TG69-42 |
| ETS alternator: | Not fitted | Brush BL100-30 |
| Number of traction motors: | 4 | 4 |
| Traction motor type: | Brush TM73-68 | Brush TM73-68 |
| Gear ratio (31101-31116): | 64 : 15 | 60 : 19 |
| (31117-31327): | 60 : 19 | — |
| Fuel tank capacity: | 530gal (2,409lit)† | 530gal (2,409lit) |
| Cooling water capacity: | 156gal (709lit) | 156gal (709lit) |
| Lubricating oil capacity: | 110gal (500lit) | 110gal (500lit) |
| Boiler water capacity: | 600gal (2,728lit)* | 600gal (2,728lit) if fitted |
| Boiler fuel capacity: | 100gal (455lit)* | 100gal (455lit) if dual* |
| Regions of allocation: | Eastern, Midland | Eastern, Midland |
| Sector ownership: | D, F | D, L, R |

\* Steam heat equipment has now been removed or isolated.
† The standard fuel tank capacity for a Class 31 is 530gal (2,409lit), however, No 31178 has extended capacity, and holds 1,230gal (5,592lit).

## Main detail variations

Locomotives 31101-112, and selectively on locomotives up to 31143 were built with the disc-style of train identification. However, progressively from 31113, and to all locomotives after 31143 a four-position, roof-mounted headcode box was fitted.

Refurbishing is now well under way, and this has led to the removal of the former waist height body band, and the installation of headlights.

31/1: Standard locomotives — originally steam heat fitted.
31/4: Locomotives fitted with Electric Train Supply (ETS).

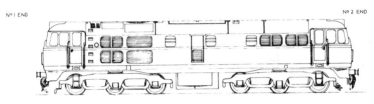

N° I END · N° 2 END

Above:
*This drawing is representative of a Class 31/1 locomotive of the batch fitted with four position route indicators. This modification was progressively adopted from No 31113 and fitted to all locomotives after No 31143.*

Below:
*Class 31 cab layout, taken from locomotive No 31200. 1. Instrument light switch, 2. Cab light switch, 3. Engine start button, 4. Engine stop button, 5. Brake pipe pressure gauge, 6. Brake cylinder gauge, 7. Vacuum gauge, 8. Ampmeter, 9. Speedometer, 10. Train brake valve, 11. Locomotive brake valve, 12. Engine stop light, 13. Wheel slip light, 14. Alarm light, 15. Power controller, 16. Master switch, 17. Position for driver's key, 18. Footwarmer switch, 19. Footwarmer switch, 20. Demister switch, 21. Main reservoir pressure gauge, 22. Driver's side windscreen wiper control, 23. AWS reset button.*
Colin J. Marsden

Below:
*Two distinct body designs exist within the Class 31 fleet — those fitted with disc (lamp) indicators, and those fitted with a roof-mounted headcode box. The upper illustration shows an original Class 31/1 from the No 1 end, driver's side, while the lower plate shows one of the later build, but this time from the No 2 end driver's side. Main equipment items are: 1. Boiler water gauge (removed on refurbished locomotives), 2. Boiler and radiator compartment, 3. Removable roof section, 4. Power unit compartment, 5. Electrical control cubicle (inside), 6. Battery box, 7. Brake cylinder, 8. Sand box, 9. Primary coil springs, 10. Secondary leaf springs, 11. Milometer.*
Both: Colin J. Marsden

Above:
*Class 31 front end layouts. Details marked on the right illustration are found in the same position on the earlier design. (Left) 1. Engine control air pipe, 2. Main reservoir pipe, 3. Air brake pipe, 4. Vacuum pipe, 5. Coupling hook, 6. Blue star multiple control jumper receptacle, 7. Blue star multiple control jumper cable, 8. Sand boxes, 9. Red 'tail' indicators, 10. Screen washers (behind), 11. Marker lights (not on earlier design). Both: Colin J. Marsden*

Below:
*The Class 31s fitted with electric train supply (ETS) are identical to the basic locomotive except for the fitting of ETS jumper and socket equipment on the front ends, and of course internal alterations. The ETS jumper is indicated on this illustration of No 31459 by the letter A, and the ETS socket by the letter B.   Colin J. Marsden*

Top:
*In common with many older classes of locomotive, refurbishing or heavy general overhaul work has been carried out to a number of Class 31s. This work has culminated in a number of visible alterations being made, including the removal of the raised bodyside band, the redesigning of the buffer beam body valance, and where appropriate the removal of headcode discs. Refurbished No 31110 is illustrated at Bristol Temple Meads.   Colin J. Marsden*

Above:
*During the refurbishing operation a number of Class 31s were fitted with high-intensity headlights. However, after some 64 locomotives had been fitted at BREL Doncaster the work was decreed a depot modification and installation ceased. Headlight-fitted No 31304, painted in Railfreight livery, is illustrated at Acton.   Colin J. Marsden*

Above:
*In 1987 a total of 23 Class 31 locomotives were fitted with snowplough brackets. However the most recent official list shows only locomotives Nos 31120/125/132/200/ 259/270/271 as actually carrying ploughs. No 31200 is illustrated. This view also shows the revised valance to the buffer beam on refurbished locomotives.* John Tuffs

Below:
*After the Railfreight livery had been applied for some 18 months a revision was made, namely the application of a red band at the base of the body, which continued around the front end. This livery variant stemmed from the red frame of the Railfreight sector's Class 58s. Class 31 No 31180 is illustrated at Doncaster Works in February 1987. Note that the BR emblem is smaller on this livery.* Colin J. Marsden

# Class 33

| Sub-Class: | 33/0 | 33/1 | 33/2 |
|---|---|---|---|
| Former Class codes: | D15/1, later 15/6 | — | D15/2, later 15/6A |
| Number range: | 33002-33065 | 33101-33119 | 33201-33212 |
| Former number range: | D6500-D6585 | Random from 33/0 fleet | D6586-D6597 |
| Built by: | Birmingham RC&W Ltd | Birmingham RC&W Ltd | Birmingham RC&W Ltd |
| Introduced: | 1960-62 | As 33/1 1965-67 | 1962 |
| Wheel arrangement: | Bo-Bo | Bo-Bo | Bo-Bo |
| Weight (operational): | 77 tonnes | 78 tonnes | 77 tonnes |
| Height: | 12ft 8in (3.86m) | 12ft 8in (3.86m) | 12ft 8in (3.86m) |
| Width: | 9ft 3in (2.81m) | 9ft 3in (2.81m) | 8ft 8in (2.64m) |
| Length: | 50ft 9in (15.47m) | 50ft 9in (15.47m) | 50ft 9in (15.47m) |
| Minimum curve negotiable: | 4 chains (80.46m) | 4 chains (80.46m) | 4 chains (80.46m) |
| Maximum speed: | 85mph (137km/h) | 85mph (137km/h) | 85mph (137km/h) |
| Wheelbase: | 39ft 0in (11.88m) | 39ft 0in (11.88m) | 39ft 0in (11.88m) |
| Bogie wheelbase: | 10ft 0in (3.04m) | 10ft 0in (3.04m) | 10ft 0in (3.04m) |
| Bogie pivot centres: | 29ft 0in (8.83m) | 29ft 0in (8.83m) | 29ft 0in (8.83m) |
| Wheel diameter: | 3ft 7in (1.09m) | 3ft 7in (1.09m) | 3ft 7in (1.09m) |
| Brake type: | Dual | Dual | Dual |
| Sanding equipment: | Pneumatic | Pneumatic | Pneumatic |
| Route availability: | 6 | 6 | 6 |
| Heating type: | Electric — Index 48* | Electric — Index 48* | Electric — Index 48* |
| Multiple coupling restriction: | Blue Star | Blue Star | Blue Star |
| Brake force: | 35 tonnes | 35 tonnes | 35 tonnes |
| Engine type: | Sulzer 8LDA28B | Sulzer 8LDA28B | Sulzer 8LDA28B |
| Engine horsepower: | 1,550hp (1,154kW) | 1,550hp (1,154kW) | 1,550hp (1,154kW) |
| Power at rail: | 1,215hp (906kW) | 1,215hp (906kW) | 1,215hp (906kW) |
| Tractive effort: | 45,000lb (200kN) | 45,000lb (200kN) | 45,000lb (200kN) |
| Cylinder bore: | 11in (0.27m) | 11in (0.27m) | 11in (0.27m) |
| Cylinder stroke: | 14in (0.35m) | 14in (0.35m) | 14in (0.35m) |
| Main generator type: | Crompton CG391-A1 | Crompton CG391-A1 | Crompton CG391-A1 |
| Auxiliary generator type: | Crompton CAG193-A1 | Crompton CAG193-A1 | Crompton CAG193-A1 |
| ETS alternator: | Crompton CAG392-A1 | Crompton CAG392-A1 | Crompton CAG392-A1 |
| Number of traction motors: | 4 | 4 | 4 |
| Traction motor type: | Crompton C171-C2 | Crompton C171-C2 | Crompton C171-C2 |

| **Gear ratio:** | 62 : 17 | 62 : 17 | 62 : 17 |
| **Fuel tank capacity:** | 750gal (3,410lit) | 750gal (3,410lit) | 750gal (3,410lit) |
| **Cooling water capacity:** | 230gal (1,046lit) | 230gal (1,046lit) | 230gal (1,046lit) |
| **Lubricating oil capacity:** | 108gal (491lit) | 108gal (491lit) | 108gal (491lit) |
| **Region of allocation:** | Southern | Southern | Southern |
| **Sector ownership:** | D, F, R, P | D, N, R | D, F |

\* The Electric Train Supply fitted to the Class 33s is designed for operation with SR-allocated 750V dc heated stock.
All locomotives are fitted with Snowplough brackets, and a number of machines are kept fitted with ploughs throughout the year.

## Subclass variations

Class 33/0: Standard locomotives.
Class 33/1: Modified locomotives, fitted with buck-eye couplers, waist height air
connections, and MU compatible jumpers. The locomotives can operate in multiple with
all post-1951 SR EMU stock.
Class 33/2: Narrow profile locomotives which were built to operate on the Hastings line,
where limited clearances prevented the use of locomotives and stock built to standard
loading gauge.

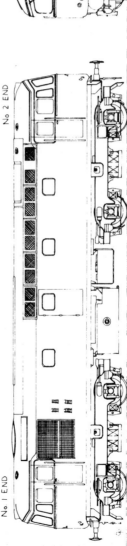

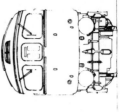

Above:
*This drawing is representative of Class 33/0 locomotives only. There
are several detail differences between this and the Class 33/1 and 33/2
sub-classes, and reference should be made to the illustrations to
establish these.*

Below and bottom:
*The Class 33/0 locomotives (Nos 33001-065) are all allocated to the SR, and have dual brakes and electric heating. These two illustrations show both sides of the locomotive; each is taken from the driver's side corner from No 1 and No 2 ends respectively. 1. No 1 end, 2. No 2 end, 3. Radiator grille, radiator unit inside, 4. Engine compartment, 5. Electric control cubicle, 6. Sand box, 7. Brake cylinder, 8. Fuel tank, 9. Battery box. For internal maintenance the engine compartment has doors in both sides, and the roof section is removable.* C. J. Tuffs; Colin J. Marsden

Right:
*The 33/1 sub-class was introduced in 1965-67, for remote operation with selected post-1951 EMUs and control trailer stock. The locomotives are fitted with a 'Westcode' control system, which enables them to be controlled while at the rear of a train via high level control jumpers. The 17 surviving members of the 33/1 sub-class are immediately recognisable by the waist height air connections and control jumpers. Locomotive No 33114 is shown from the No 2 end at Stewarts Lane.* Colin J. Marsden

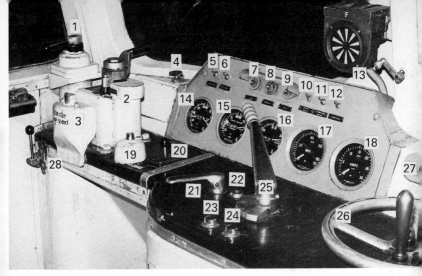

Above:

*Class 33 cab layout, applicable to Classes 33/0 and 33/2. Locomotives of Class 33/1 have revised engine start and stop switch gear. 1. Locomotive brake valve, 2. Train brake valve, 3. Exhauster (vacuum) high speed button, 4. Driver's window wiper valve, 5. Route indicator light switch, 6. Instrument light switch, 7. Engine stopped light, 8. Wheelslip warning light, 9. Fault light, 10. Driver's side heat switch, 11. Driver's assistant's side heat switch, 12. Demister switch, 13. AWS indicator, 14. Main reservoir-train pipe pressure gauge, 15. Brake cylinder pressure gauge, 16. Vacuum gauge, 17. Speedometer, 18. Ampmeter, 19. AWS reset button, 20. Warning horn valve, 21. Master switch (OFF/REV/EO/FOR), 22. Master key socket, 23. Engine start button, 24. Engine stop button, 25. Power controller, 26. Handbrake wheel, 27. ETS 'on' button, 28. Sanding valve.*   Colin J. Marsden

This page:
*Front end detail of Class 33/0 (top left), Class 33/1 (top right) and Class 33/2 (right). 1. Engine control air pipe, 2. ETS jumper socket, 3. Main reservoir pipe, 4. Multiple control jumper sockets (jumper stored inside locomotive), 5. Vacuum pipe, 6. Screw coupling, 7. Air brake pipe, 8. ETS jumper cable, 9. Red/white marker light (disconnected), 10. Buck-eye coupling, 11. Waist height jumper cable, 12. Waist height main reservoir pipe, 13. Waist height brake pipe, 14. Waist height multiple control jumper (EMU), 15. Power socket for Weymouth Quay flashing light, 16. AWS receiver, 17. Snowplough brackets.*
Colin J. Marsden (2), Martin Searle (1)

Above:
*In June 1986 Eastleigh Works repainted No 33008* Eastleigh *into BR green livery. At first the locomotive had a full yellow end, but by the end of the year depot staff returned the locomotive to what was virtually mid-1960s condition, with small yellow warning panels, and the lion and wheel crests. No 33008* Eastleigh *is illustrated in the works yard at BREL Eastleigh on 12 October 1986.* Colin J. Marsden

Below:
*All Class 33s have snowplough brackets; however, only 23 locomotives actually carried ploughs during 1988. The ploughs are of the standard three-piece miniature type, and are usually painted yellow. No 33032 (now withdrawn) passes New Malden showing the snowplough fitment.* Colin J. Marsden

# Class 37

| Sub-Class: | 37/0 | 37/3 | 37/4 |
|---|---|---|---|
| Former Class codes: | D17/1, later 17/3 | — | — |
| Number range: | 37001-37326 | 37350-37381 | 37401-37431 |
| Former number range: | D6600-D6999 | From main fleet | From main fleet |
| Built by: | EE & RSH Ltd | EE & RSH Ltd | EE |
| Introduced: | 1960-65 | As 37/3 — 1988 | As 37/4 1985-86 |
| Wheel arrangement: | Co-Co | Co-Co | Co-Co |
| Weight (operational): | 102-108 tonnes | 106 tonnes | 107 tonnes |
| Height: | 12ft 9$\frac{1}{16}$in (3.89m) | 12ft 9$\frac{1}{16}$in (3.89m) | 12ft 9$\frac{1}{16}$in (3.89m) |
| Width: | 8ft 10⅜in (2.70m) | 8ft 10⅜in (2.70m) | 8ft 10⅜in (2.70m) |
| Length: | 61ft 6in (18.74m) | 61ft 6in (18.74m) | 61ft 6in (18.74m) |
| Minimum curve negotiable: | 4 chains (80.46m) | 4 chains (80.46m) | 4 chains (80.46m) |
| Maximum speed: | 80mph (129km/h) | 80mph (129km/h) | 80mph (129km/h) |
| Wheelbase: | 50ft 8in (15.44m) | 50ft 8in (15.44m) | 50ft 8in (15.44m) |
| Bogie wheelbase: | 13ft 6in (4.11m) | 13ft 6in (4.11m) | 13ft 6in (4.11m) |
| Bogie pivot centres: | 37ft 2in (11.32m) | 37ft 2in (11.32m) | 37ft 2in (11.32m) |
| Wheel diameter (driving): | 3ft 9in (1.14m) | 3ft 9in (1.14m) | 3ft 9in (1.14m) |
| Brake type: | Dual | Dual | Dual |
| Sanding equipment: | Pneumatic | Pneumatic | Pneumatic |
| Heating type: | Steam[2] | Not fitted | Electric — Index 3 |
| Train heat alternator: | Not fitted | Not fitted | Brush BAH 701 |
| Route availability: | 5 | 5 | 5 |
| Coupling restriction: | Blue Star | Blue Star | Blue Star |
| Brake force: | 50 tonnes | 50 tonnes | 50 tonnes |
| Engine type: | EE 12 CSVT | EE 12 CSVT | EE 12 CSVT |
| Engine horsepower: | 1,750hp (1,304kW) | 1,750hp (1,304kW) | 1,750hp (1,304kW) |
| Power at rail: | 1,250hp (932kW) | 1,250hp (932kW) | 1,250hp (932kW) |
| Tractive effort: | 55,000lb (247kN) | 55,000lb (247kN) | 55,000lb (247kN) |
| Cylinder bore: | 10in (0.25m) | 10in (0.25m) | 10in (0.25m) |
| Cylinder stroke: | 12in (0.30m) | 12in (0.30m) | 12in (0.30m) |
| Main generator type: | EE 822/10G | EE 822/10G | Not fitted |
| Traction alternator type: | Not fitted | Not fitted | Brush BA 100SA |
| Auxiliary generator type: | EE 911/5C | EE 911/5C | Not fitted |
| Number of traction motors: | 6 | 6 | 6 |
| Traction motor type: | EE 538/1A | EE 538/1A | EE 538/1A |
| Gear ratio: | 53 : 18 | 53 : 18 | 53 : 18 |
| Fuel tank capacity[3]: | 890gal (4,046lit) | 1,690gal (7,682lit) | 1,690gal (7,682lit) |
| Cooling water capacity: | 160gal (727lit) | 160gal (727lit) | 160gal (727lit) |
| Boiler water capacity: | 800gal (3,637lit) | Not fitted | Not fitted |
| Lubricating oil capacity: | 120gal (545lit) | 120gal (545lit) | 120gal (545lit) |
| Boiler fuel capacity: | From main supply | Not fitted | Not fitted |
| Region of allocation: | Eastern, Western, Scottish | Eastern, Western | Western, Scottish |
| Sector ownership: | D, F, L | F, L | P, D, F, I |

Notes:

[1] Locomotives renumbered between 37501-37540 are refurbished phase 1 locomotives, from the original number range 37001-37119, and are fitted with Brush BA100SA alternators, while those numbered between 37575-37599 are refurbished phase 1 locomotives fitted with GEC G564 alternators.
Locomotives renumbered 37600-37624 are refurbished phase 2 locomotives, from the original series 37120-37308, and are fitted with GEC 564 alternators, while those numbered between 37650-37699 are fitted with Brush BA100SA alternators.

[2] Steam heating is now almost a thing of the past, with only a handful of boiler-fitted examples remaining in traffic.

[3] As locomotives are refurbished, the existing boiler water tanks are being converted into additional fuel tanks, doubling the locomotives' operating range.

| 37/5[1] | 37/7[4] | 37/9 | 37/9 |
|---|---|---|---|
| — | — | — | — |
| 37501-37699 | 37701-37899 | 37901-37904 | 37905-37906 |
| From main fleet | From main fleet | From main fleet | From main fleet |
| EE & RSH Ltd | EE & RSH Ltd | EE & RSH Ltd | EE Ltd |
| As 37/5 — 1986- | As 37/7 — 1986- | As 37/9 — 1986-87 | As 37/9 — 1987 |
| Co-Co | Co-Co | Co-Co | Co-Co |
| 107 tonnes | 120 tonnes | 120 tonnes | 120 tonnes |
| 12ft 9¹⁄₁₆in (3.89m) | 12ft 9¹⁄₁₆in (3.89m) | 12ft 9¹⁄₁₆in (3.89m) | 12ft 9¹⁄₁₆in (3.89m) |
| 8ft 10⅜in (2.70m) | 8ft 10⅜in (2.70m) | 8ft 10⅜in (2.70m) | 8ft 10⅜in (2.70m) |
| 61ft 6in (18.74m) | 61ft 6in (18.74m) | 61ft 6in (18.74m) | 61ft 6in (18.74m) |
| 4 chains (80.46m) | 4 chains (80.46m) | 4 chains (80.46m) | 4 chains (80.46m) |
| 80mph (129km/h) | 80mph (129km/h) | 80mph (129km/h) | 80mph (129km/h) |
| 50ft 8in (15.44m) | 50ft 8in (15.44m) | 50ft 8in (15.44m) | 50ft 8in (15.44m) |
| 13ft 6in (4.11m) | 13ft 6in (4.11m) | 13ft 6in (4.11m) | 13ft 6in (4.11m) |
| 37ft 2in (11.32m) | 37ft 2in (11.32m) | 37ft 2in (11.32m) | 37ft 2in (11.32m) |
| 3ft 9in (1.14m) | 3ft 9in (1.14m) | 3ft 9in (1.14m) | 3ft 9in (1.14m) |
| Dual | Dual | Dual | Dual |
| Pneumatic | Pneumatic | Pneumatic | Pneumatic |
| Not fitted | Not fitted | Not fitted | Not fitted |
| Not fitted | Not fitted | Not fitted | Not fitted |
| 5 | 7 | 7 | 7 |
| Blue Star | Blue Star | Blue Star | Blue Star |
| — | — | 50 tonnes | 50 tonnes |
| EE 12 CSVT | EE 12 CSVT | Mirrlees MB 275T | Ruston RK 270T |
| 1,750hp (1,304kW) | 1,750hp (1,304kW) | 1,800hp (1,340kW) | 1,800hp (1,340kW) |
| 1,250hp (247kW) | 1,250hp (247kW) | — | — |
| 55,000lb (247kN) | 55,000lb (247kN) | — | — |
| 10in (0.25m) | 10in (0.25m) | — | — |
| 12in (0.30m) | 12in (0.30m) | — | — |
| Not fitted | Not fitted | Not fitted | Not fitted |
| 1 | 4 | Brush 100SA | GEC 564 |
| Not fitted | Not fitted | Not fitted | Not fitted |
| 6 | 6 | 6 | 6 |
| EE 538/1A | EE 538/1A | EE 538/1A | EE 538/1A |
| 53 : 18 | 53 : 18 | 53 : 18 | 53 : 18 |
| 1,690gal (7,682lit) | 1,690gal (7,682lit) | 1,690gal (7,682lit) | 1,690gal (7,682lit) |
| 160gal (727lit) | 160gal (727lit) | — | — |
| Not fitted | Not fitted | Not fitted | Not fitted |
| 120gal (545lit) | 120gal (545lit) | — | — |
| Not fitted | Not fitted | Not fitted | Not fitted |
| Western, Eastern | Western, Eastern | Western | Western |
| F | F | F | F |

[4] Locomotives renumbered between 37701-37714, are refurbished phase 1 locomotives, from the original batch 37001-37119, and are now fitted with Brush BA100SA alternators; locomotives renumbered 37788-37799 are the same but fitted with GEC G564 alternators. Locomotives renumbered 37800-37813, are refurbished phase 2 locomotives from the original batch, 37120-37308, that are fitted with GEC G564 alternators, while locomotives numbered 37884-37899 are the same but fitted with Brush BA100SA alternators.

## Subclass variations

Class 37/0: Standard locomotive.
Class 37/3: Unrefurbished Class 37/0 fitted with new CP7 bogies for 'Railfreight' sector.
Class 37/4: Electric Train Supply (ETS) modified locomotives.
Class 37/5: Refurbished 'Railfreight' sector locomotive with Route Availability of 5, some locomotives fitted with slow speed control.
Class 37/7: Refurbished 'Railfreight' sector locomotive with Route Availability of 7, fitted with slow speed control, and ballast weights.
Class 37/9: Refurbished 'Railfreight' sector locomotive, fitted with experimental power units.

Under the original numbering system phase 1 locomotives Nos 37001-37119 were built with split route indicator boxes, ie two characters either side of a central gangway door. Phase 2 locomotives Nos 37120-37308 were built with a four-character central headcode box.
Under the refurbishing scheme, locomotives with split headcode boxes will have them removed and marker lights installed in their place, while locomotives with a central headcode box will retain the fitment but have it plated over and two marker lights fitted centrally.

Below:
*Class 37 cab layout: 1. Train brake valve, 2. Locomotive brake valve, 3. Windscreen wiper valve, 4. Windscreen wiper motor, 5. Engine stop light, 6. Wheelslip light, 7. Fault light, 8. Indicator dimmer switch, 9. AWS reset button, 10. AWS indicator, 11. Nose light, 12. Cab heat switch, 13. Cab heat switch, 14. Sanding button, 15. Engine start button, 16. Engine stop button, 17. Speedometer, 18. Ampmeter, 19. Brake pipe gauge, 20. Vacuum gauge, 21. Brake cylinder pressure gauge, 22. Horn valve, 23. Master switch, 24. Power controller, 25. Main reservoir gauge.   Colin J. Marsden*

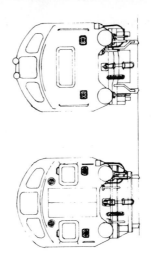

**Above:**

*There are two distinct body designs in the Class 37 fleet. Locomotives Nos 37.001-119 are fitted with split route indicator boxes, formerly each side of a central gangway door, whilst the remainder of the fleet have solid central route indicator boxes. The front end valance behind the buffer beams are in the course of modification being straightened at buffer beam level. This side elevation is of a locomotive in the number range 37.001-119, with the two different front end designs both shown.*

*Class 37 front end layout. The four styles of Class 37 front end layout are all shown on this page, the two lower illustrations indicate the equipment, which can be found in the same position on all types. (Top left) Class 37/0, (top right) Class 37/0, (bottom left) Class 37/4, (bottom right) Class 37/5. (Applicable to 37/7, and 37/9). 1. Marker lights, 2. High intensity headlight, 3. Engine control air pipe, 4. Main reservoir pipe, 5. Multiple control jumper socket, 6. Vacuum pipe, 7. Coupling, 8. Air brake pipe, 9. Multiple control jumper cable, 10. Snowplough brackets, 11. Red 'tail' lights, 12. ETS cable, 13. ETS socket. Note: the top right illustration shows the RETB aerial in the bonnet top.*
Colin J. Marsden (3), Brian Morrison (1)

Below:

*As detailed in the introductory text, two front end designs exist within the Class 37 fleet. These two illustrations show both sides of a standard Class 37/0 locomotive, both are taken from the No 1 end, and show the two front styles. 1. Traction motor blower and air compressor compartment, 2. Radiator compartment, 3. Engine and generator compartment, 4. Boiler compartment, 5. Electrical cubicle, 6. Removable roof section, 7. Brake cylinder (3 per bogie side), 8. Fuel tank, 9. Traction motor blower and vacuum exhauster compartment, 10. Sand box filler ports.* Both: Colin J. Marsden

Top:
*The 16 locomotives of Class 37/0 (Nos 37350-381) were converted for use by the Railfreight Sector on British Steel traffic. Most of the locomotives carry steel-associated names, and have had their vacuum exhausters isolated, making them air brake-only locomotives. Locomotives 37350-381 are being renumbered in the conventional 37/0 series.* Tom Noble

Above:
*Major refurbishing of Class 37 locomotives commenced in 1985, when work started on a fleet of 31 ETS fitted locomotives (Class 37/4). The work involved was considerable with only the shell of the original locomotive being used. Major electrical work was also carried out, including the installation of ac alternators in place of dc generators. Externally the most noticeable change was the alteration to nose end grilles on the driver's assistant's side, and the installation of larger fire pulls at both ends. No 37405 is illustrated at BREL Crewe soon after completion.* Colin J. Marsden

Above:
*The Class 37/4 locomotives are all painted in 'more yellow' livery style, and are allocated to Eastfield, Inverness and Cardiff, where they are operated by the Freight, Provincial Parcels, Departmental and InterCity sectors. A number of the 37/4s have been named. No 37430* Cwmbran *is illustrated. Locomotives Nos 37414-421 are fitted with Radio Electronic Token Block (RETB) equipment, and have an aerial on the centre of the nose, for use in Scotland.* John Tuffs

Below:
*The Class 37/5s are straightforward refurbished Railfreight sector locomotives, with a route availability of 5. External alterations are similar to those effected for the Class 37/4s, but locomotives from the earlier split headcode box fleet have had the boxes removed, and two sealed beam headlights fitted. The former nose-end doors have of course been plated over. No 37501 is illustrated on the WR main line with a 'Speedlink' coal duty.* Colin J. Marsden

Below:
*Locomotives Nos 37650-699 are fitted with Brush BA100SA alternators and have been rebuilt from the original phase 2 batch, ie those with a central route panel. No 37689 (formerly No 37195) is illustrated at Crewe. All refurbished Class 37s are fitted with headlights and snowplough brackets, and are equipped for single manning.* John Tuffs

Bottom:
*In February 1987 Class 37/5 No 37501 was outshopped by Thornaby depot in British Steel livery, bearing the British Steel logo. No 37501, running in multiple with No 37506, passes Toton with a Lackenby-Corby steel train.* John Tuffs

**Above:**

*Locomotives classified 37/7 are refurbished examples which are similar to Class 37/5s but have ballast weights added to improve adhesion. Most are also fitted with slow speed control equipment. Reference should be made to the introductory text regarding batch conversions. Externally there is no difference between Classes 37/5 and 37/7. No 37898, which is a refurbished phase 2 locomotive fitted with Brush electrical equipment, is seen passing the now closed Ebbw Junction depot.   Colin J. Marsden*

**Below:**

*In April 1987 a further revision to the 'Railfreight' livery was introduced, when a red band was applied the complete way around the lower edge of the locomotive. This livery variation is illustrated on Class 37/5 No 37517 at BREL Crewe — this being a refurbished phase 1 locomotive on which the former split route boxes have been removed.   Brian Morrison*

Top:
*To provide facilities for the trial of new power units BR made six Class 37s available to Mirrlees (four) and GEC-Ruston (two). These six locomotives were refurbished at BREL Crewe at BR's expense, and fitted out at the manufacturer's expense with new trial power equipment. All six locomotives are painted in Railfreight grey livery and are allocated to Cardiff. No external differences exist between the Class 37/9s and other refurbished Class 37s. No 37906 is illustrated passing Llanwern with a steel train for BSC Ebbw Vale.* Colin J. Marsden

Above:
*Today a number of Class 37s carry nameplates, and in many cases these reflect industries that have supported BR over the years. One such company is British Steel, who produce thousands of tonnes of steel for shipment each week, and in return have a number of locomotives with affiliated names. Class 37/0 No 37226 carries the name* The Cardiff Rod Mill, *together with a steel and Welsh dragon crest above.*
Colin J. Marsden

Above:
*All refurbished Class 37s and a handful of Class 37/0s and 37/3s have snowplough brackets. However, like other classes, only a few actually carry the three-piece miniature ploughs at any one time. Scottish allocated No 37085 shows the snowplough fitment in this illustration at Glasgow. This locomotive was also sporting a headlight.*
Colin J. Marsden

Below:
*Following the introduction of Railfreight Sub-Sector liveries in October 1987, several members of this class have emerged in the 'double grey' scheme. Sporting the Petroleum Sub-Sector motif, No 37893 of Stratford allocation, is illustrated at Ripple Lane.* Colin J. Marsden

# Class 40

| | |
|---|---|
| **Former Class code:** | D20/1, later 20/3 |
| **Number:** | 40122 (D200)* |
| **Former number range:** | D200-D399 |
| **Built by:** | EE Ltd |
| **Introduced:** | 1958 |
| **Wheel arrangement:** | 1Co-Co1 |
| **Weight (operational):** | 136 tonnes |
| **Height:** | 12ft 10in (3.91m) |
| **Width:** | 9ft 0in (2.74m) |
| **Length:** | 96ft 6in (21.18m) |
| **Minimum curve negotiable:** | 4½ chains (90.52m) |
| **Maximum speed:** | 90mph (145km/h) |
| **Wheelbase:** | 61ft 3in (18.66m) |
| **Bogie wheelbase:** | 21ft 6in (6.55m) |
| **Bogie pivot centres:** | 34ft 4in (10.46m) |
| **Wheel diameter (driving):** | 3ft 9in (1.14m) |
| **(pony):** | 3ft 0in (0.91m) |
| **Brake type:** | Dual |
| **Sanding equipment:** | Pneumatic |
| **Heating type:** | Steam — Stones OK 4625 |
| **Route availability:** | 6 |
| **Multiple coupling restriction:** | Blue Star |
| **Brake force:** | 51 tonnes |
| **Engine type:** | English Electric 16SVT Mk 11 |
| **Engine horsepower:** | 2,000hp (1,490kW) |
| **Power at rail:** | 1,550hp (1,160kW) |
| **Tractive effort:** | 52,000lb (231kN) |
| **Cylinder bore:** | 10in (0.25m) |
| **Cylinder stroke:** | 12in (0.30m) |
| **Main generator type:** | EE822 |
| **Auxiliary generator type:** | EE911-2B |
| **Number of traction motors:** | 6 |
| **Traction motor type:** | EE526-5D |
| **Gear ratio:** | 61 : 19 |
| **Fuel tank capacity:** | 710gal (3,228lit) |
| **Cooling water capacity:** | 200gal (909lit) |
| **Boiler water capacity:** | 200gal (909lit) |
| **Lubricating oil capacity:** | 140gal (636lit) |
| **Region of allocation:** | Midland |
| **Sector ownership:** | I |

* 40122 (formerly D200) was retained by BR for the operation of BR enthusiasts' specials, as well as normal traffic requirements until 16 April 1988. The livery applied being BR green, with full yellow ends.

The technical specification given above is only relevant to No D200, since withdrawn and now housed in the National Railway Museum, York.

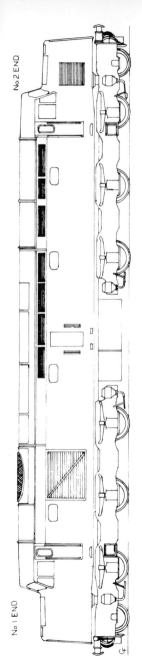

No.2 END

No.1 END

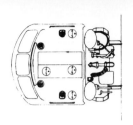

**Above:**
*D200 (40122) in original condition, as built by English Electric at Vulcan foundry in March 1958.* GEC Traction Ltd

59

Above:
*The once 200-strong Class 40 fleet now consists of just one locomotive, No 40122 or D200. The locomotive was restored by BR to original green livery in 1983 and operated by the InterCity sector until withdrawal in May 1988. These two illustrations show both sides of the locomotive — the upper illustration is from the No 1 end, while the lower is from the No 2. The two body sides are virtually identical except for revision to cant rail ventilation grilles. The upper illustration shows No 40122 at Carlisle, while the lower shows the locomotive at Linby.* Colin J. Marsden, John Tuffs

Above:

*Class 40 cab layout: 1. Train brake valve, 2. Locomotive brake valve, 3. Windscreen wiper control, 4. Windscreen wiper motor, 5. Speedometer, 6. Brake pipe pressure gauge, 7. Ampmeter, 8. Vacuum gauge, 9. Main reservoir gauge, 10. Bogie brake cylinder gauge, 11. Engine stopped warning light, 12. Wheelslip warning light, 13. Fault light, 14. Indicator dimmer switch, 15. AWS reset button, 16. AWS indicator, 17. Sanding button, 18. Engine start button, 19. Engine stop button, 20. Nose light, 21. Cab heater, 22. Cab heater, 23. Power controller, 24. Master switch, 25. Horn valve, 26. Screen wash control.* Colin J. Marsden

Below:

*Class 40 front end layout: 1. Body/bogie control connection, 2. Engine control air pipe, 3. Main reservoir pipe, 4. Blue-star multiple control jumper socket, 5. Blue-star multiple control jumper cable, 6. Vacuum pipe, 7. Coupling, 8. Air brake pipe, 9. Steam heat pipe, 10. Air warning horns (behind grille), 11. Red 'tail' indicators, 12. Front marker lights and discs.* John Tuffs

# Class 45

| Sub-Class: | 45/0 | 45/1 |
|---|---|---|
| Former Class codes: | D25/1, later 25/1 | D25/1, later 25/1 |
| Present number range: | 45007-45052 | 45103-45141 |
| Former number range: | D11-137[1] | D11-137[1] |
| Built by: | BR Derby & Crewe | BR Derby & Crewe |
| Introduced: | 1960-62 | As 45/1 1973-75 |
| Wheel arrangement: | 1Co-Co1 | 1Co-Co1 |
| Weight (operational): | 138 tonnes | 135 tonnes |
| Height: | 12ft 10⅛in (3.91m) | 12ft 10⅛in (3.91m) |
| Width: | 8ft 10⅝in (2.70m) | 8ft 10⅝in (2.70m) |
| Length: | 67ft 11in (20.70m) | 67ft 11in (20.70m) |
| Minimum curve negotiable: | 5 chains (100.58m) | 5 chains (100.58m) |
| Maximum speed: | 90mph (145km/h) | 90mph (145km/h) |
| Wheelbase: | 59ft 8in (18.18m) | 59ft 8in (18.18m) |
| Bogie wheelbase: | 21ft 6in (6.55m) | 21ft 6in (6.55m) |
| Bogie pivot centres: | 32ft 8in (9.95m) | 32ft 8in (9.95m) |
| Wheel diameter (driving): | 3ft 9in (1.14m) | 3ft 9in (1.14m) |
| (pony): | 3ft 0in (0.91m) | 3ft 0in (0.91m) |
| Brake type: | Dual | Dual |
| Sanding equipment: | Pneumatic | Pneumatic |
| Heating type: | Steam — Stones OK 4625[2] | Electric — Index 66 |
| Route availability: | 7 | 6 |
| Multiple coupling restriction: | Not multiple fitted | Not multiple fitted |
| Brake force: | 63 tonnes | 63 tonnes |
| Engine type: | Sulzer 12LDA28B | Sulzer 12LDA28B |
| Engine horsepower: | 2,500hp (1,862kW) | 2,500hp (1,862kW) |
| Power at rail: | 2,000hp (1,490kW) | 2,000hp (1,490kW) |
| Tractive effort: | 55,000lb (245kN) | 55,000lb (245kN) |
| Cylinder bore: | 11in (0.27m) | 11in (0.27m) |
| Cylinder stroke: | 14in (0.35m) | 14in (0.35m) |
| Main generator type: | Crompton CG462A1 | Crompton CG462A1 |
| Auxiliary generator type: | Crompton CAG252A1 | Crompton CAG252A1 |
| ETS alternator: | Not fitted | Brush BL 100-30 Mk 11 |
| Number of traction motors: | 6 | 6 |
| Traction motor type: | Crompton C172A1 | Crompton C172A1 |
| Gear ratio: | 62 : 17 | 62 : 17 |
| Fuel tank capacity: | 790gal (3,591lit) | 790gal (3,591lit) |
| Cooling water capacity: | 346gal (1,572lit) | 346gal (1,572lit) |
| Lubricating oil capacity: | 190gal (864lit) | 190gal (864lit) |
| Boiler water capacity: | 1,040gal (4,727lit) | Not fitted |
| Boiler fuel capacity: | From main supply | Not fitted |
| Region of allocation: | Eastern | Eastern |
| Sector ownership: | D | R |

*Notes:*

[1] The renumbering of the Class 45s was carried out as locomotives passed through works for overhaul and does not reflect their original numbers in any way.

[2] Steam heat is now extinct on this class.

[3] Class 45 will be withdrawn by 10 July, except No 45110 which is retained for InterCity charter work.

Right:
*Class 45 front end layouts. Class 45/0 (left), Class 45/1 (right). 1. Sealed beam marker lights, 2. Red 'tail' indicators, 3. Main reservoir pipe, 4. Air brake pipe, 5. Steam pipe (isolated), 6. Vacuum pipe, 7. Coupling, 8. Jumper socket, 9. ETS jumper cable, 10. High-intensity headlight.* John Tuffs, Colin J. Marsden

## Subclass variations

Class 45/0: Basic locomotive, fitted with steam heat equipment (now isolated), Route Availability 6.

Class 45/1: Electric Train Supply (ETS) fitted locomotive, Route Availability 7.

When introduced, two types of front end headcode display were fitted. The split headcode box, or the solid central panel-type box. All surviving locomotives have now had the headcode boxes removed in favour of marker lights, and the majority now sport headlights.

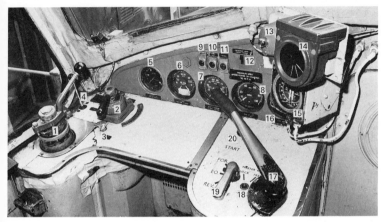

Above:
*Class 45 cab layout: 1. Train brake valve, 2. Locomotive brake valve, 3. Windscreen wiper valve, 4. Horn valve, 5. Brake pipe gauge, 6. Vacuum gauge, 7. Brake cylinder gauge, 8. Speedometer, 9. Engine stopped light, 10. Wheel slip light, 11. Fault light, 12. Instrument light switch, 13. AWS reset button, 14. AWS indicator, 15. Main reservoir gauge, 16. Ampmeter, 17. Power controller, 18. Key socket, 19. Master switch, 20. Start switch.* Colin J. Marsden

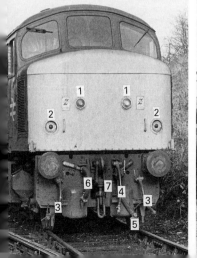

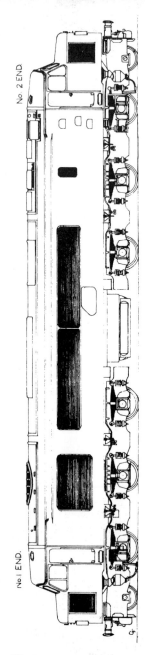

No 2 END

No I END.

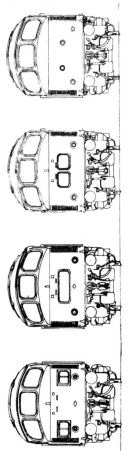

Above:
Two distinct types of Class 45 are in service — 45/0 locomotives were originally fitted with steam heat equipment, and 45/1 have the electric train heat system. This side elevation represents a Class 45/0. Four different front ends are shown: When built Nos D11-D31 and D68-D107 were fitted with split four position headcode boxes, two each side of a central gangway position. The remainder of the fleet were either fitted with a two-piece or solid central four position headcode. Following a decision to dispense with headcodes during the 1970s, the Class 45s had their front ends remodelled to accommodate two fixed beam headlights in the former headcode position.

The Class 45 or 'Peak' Class locomotives were first introduced in 1960 but are scheduled for early withdrawal. The fleet is divided into two sub-classes — 45/0 (steam or no heat fitted) and 45/1 (Electric Train Supply fitted). These two illustrations show the two different sub-classes — both views are taken from the No 2 end and show the two different sides of the locomotives. Main equipment areas are: A, No 2 end, B, No 1 end, 1. Traction motor blower compartment, 2. Train heat, or ETS compartment, 3. Main/auxiliary generator compartment, 4. Power unit position, 5. Brake frame and compressor compartment, 6. Radiator compartment, 7. Fuel tanks, 8. Battery box, 9. Air reservoirs.   Both: Colin J. Marsden

# Class 47

| | | |
|---|---|---|
| **Sub-Class:** | 47/0 | 47/3 |
| **Former Class codes:** | 27/2 | 27/2 |
| **Present number range:** | 47002-47299 | 47301-47381 |
| **Former number range:** | D1521-D1998[1] | D1782-D1900 |
| **Built by:** | BR Crewe, Brush Ltd | BR Crewe, Brush Ltd |
| **Introduced:** | 1962-65 | 1964-65 |
| **Wheel arrangement:** | Co-Co | Co-Co |
| **Weight (operational):** | 111-121 tonnes | 114 tonnes |
| **Height:** | 12ft 9⅜in (3.89m) | 12ft 9⅜in (3.89m) |
| **Width:** | 9ft 2in (2.79m) | 9ft 2in (2.79m) |
| **Length:** | 63ft 7in (19.38m) | 63ft 7in (19.38m) |
| **Minimum curve negotiable:** | 4 chains (80.46m) | 4 chains (80.46m) |
| **Maximum speed:** | 95mph (153km/h)[11] | 95mph (153km/h)[11] |
| **Wheelbase:** | 51ft 6in (15.69m) | 51ft 6in (15.69m) |
| **Bogie wheelbase:** | 14ft 6in (4.41m) | 14ft 6in (4.41m) |
| **Bogie pivot centres:** | 37ft 0in (11.27m) | 37ft 0in (11.27m) |
| **Wheel diameter (driving):** | 3ft 9in (1.14m) | 3ft 9in (1.14m) |
| **Brake type:** | Dual | Dual |
| **Sanding equipment:** | Not fitted | Not fitted |
| **Heating type:** | Steam[5] | Not fitted |
| **Route availability:** | 6 | 6 |
| **Coupling restriction:** | Not fitted | Not fitted |
| **Brake force:** | 60 tonnes | 60 tonnes |
| **Engine type:** | Sulzer 12LDA28C | Sulzer 12LDA28C |
| **Engine horsepower:** | 2,580hp (1,922kW) | 2,580hp (1,922kW) |
| **Power at rail:** | 2,080hp (1,550kW) | 2,080hp (1,550kW) |
| **Tractive effort:** | 60,000lb (267kN) | 60,000lb (267kN) |
| **Cylinder bore:** | 11in (0.27m) | 11in (0.27m) |
| **Cylinder stroke:** | 14in (0.35m) | 14in (0.35m) |
| **Main generator type:** | Brush TG160-60 or TG172-50 | Brush TG160-60 or TG172-50 |
| **Main alternator type:** | Not fitted | Not fitted |
| **Auxiliary generator type:** | Brush TG69-20 or TG69-28 | Brush TG69-20 or TG69-28 |
| **Auxiliary alternator type:** | Not fitted | Not fitted |
| **ETS generator:** | Not fitted | Not fitted |
| **ETS alternator:** | Not fitted | Not fitted |
| **Number of traction motors:** | 6 | 6 |
| **Traction motor type:** | Brush TM64-68 | Brush TM64-68 |
| **Gear ratio:** | 66 : 17 | 66 : 17 |
| **Fuel tank capacity:** | 765gal (3,477lit) | 765gal (3,477lit) |
| **Cooling water capacity:** | 300gal (1,364lit) | 300gal (1,364lit) |
| **Boiler water capacity:** | 1,250gal (5,683lit) | Not fitted |
| **Lubricating oil capacity:** | 190gal (864lit) | 190gal (864lit) |
| **Boiler fuel capacity:** | From main supply | Not fitted |
| **Region of allocation:** | Eastern, Midland, Scottish, Western | Eastern, Midland, Western |
| **Sector ownership:** | F, L, D | F, L, D |

| 47/4 | 47/7 | 47/9 |
|---|---|---|
| 27/2 | — | — |
| 47401-47665 | 47701-47716 | 47901 |
| [2] | [3] | D1628 (47046) |
| BR Crewe, Brush Ltd | BR Crewe, Brush Ltd | BR Crewe |
| [4] | As 47/7 1979, 1984 | As 47/9 — 1979 |
| Co-Co | Co-Co | Co-Co |
| 120-125 tonnes | 119 tonnes | 117 tonnes |
| 12ft 9⅜in (3.89m) | 12ft 9⅜in (3.89m) | 12ft 9⅜in (3.89m) |
| 9ft 2in (2.79m) | 9ft 2in (2.79m) | 9ft 2in (2.79m) |
| 63ft 7in (19.38m) | 63ft 7in (19.38m) | 63ft 7in (19.38m) |
| 4 chains (80.46m) | 4 chains (80.46m) | 4 chains (80.46m) |
| 95mph (153km/h) | 100mph (161km/h) | 80mph (129km/h) |
| 51ft 6in (15.69m) | 51ft 6in (15.69m) | 51ft 6in (15.69m) |
| 14ft 6in (4.41m) | 14ft 6in (4.41m) | 14ft 6in (4.41m) |
| 37ft 0in (11.27m) | 37ft 0in (11.27m) | 37ft 0in (11.27m) |
| 3ft 9in (1.14m) | 3ft 9in (1.14m) | 3ft 9in (1.14m) |
| Dual | Dual | Air |
| Not fitted | Not fitted | Pneumatic |
| Electric — Index 66 | Electric — Index 66 | Not fitted |
| [6] | [7] | [6] |
| Not fitted | Not fitted | Not fitted |
| 60 tonnes | 60 tonnes | 60 tonnes |
| Sulzer 12LDA28C | Sulzer 12LDA28C | Ruston Paxman 12RK3CT |
| 2,580hp (1,922kW) | 2,580hp (1,922kW) | 3,300hp (2,455kW) |
| 2,080hp (1,550kW) | 2,080hp (1,550kW) | 2,808hp (2,089kW) |
| 60,000lb (267kN)[6] | 60,000lb (267kN) | 57,325lb (255kN) |
| 11in (0.27m) | 11in (0.27m) | 10in (0.25m) |
| 14in (0.35m) | 14in (0.35m) | 12in (0.30m) |
| Brush TG160-60 or TG172-50 | Brush TG160-60 or TG172-50 | Not fitted |
| Not fitted | Not fitted | |
| Brush TG69-20 or TG69-28 | Brush TG69-20 or TG69-28 | Brush BA 1101A |
| Not fitted | Not fitted | Not fitted |
| [7] | Not fitted | |
| [8] | Not fitted | Brush BAA602A |
| | Brush BL100-30 | Not fitted |
| [6] | [6] | Not fitted |
| Brush TM64-68 | Brush TM64-68 | [6] |
| 66 : 17 | 66 : 17 | Brush TM64-68 Mk 1A |
| [9] | 1,380gal (6,273lit) | 66 : 17 |
| 300gal (1,364lit) | 300gal (1,364lit) | 765gal (3,477lit) |
| [10] | Not fitted | 300gal (1,364lit) |
| 190gal (864lit) | 190gal (864lit) | Not fitted |
| [10] | Not fitted | 190gal (864lit) |
| | | Not fitted |
| Eastern, Midland, Scottish, Western | Scottish | Western |
| I, R, D, F, L, P, N | P | F |

*Notes:*
1. The Class 47/0 fleet were renumbered in order from Nos D1521-D1998, at the time of the introduction of TOPS in 1974; since then a number of locomotives have been converted to Electric Train Supply (ETS), and altered to Class 47/4.
2. The Class 47/4 fleet of ETS-fitted locomotives, were renumbered in sequence with the introduction of TOPS in 1974; since then a considerable number of further ETS conversions have taken place, which has led to the present numbers being largely out of sequence with the original numbers.
3. The Class 47/7s were renumbered from Class 47/4s upon conversion.
4. The first purpose-built ETS Class 47/4s emerged in 1962; in more recent years, conversions of steam heat Class 47/0s has taken place, continuing until 1987.
5. The majority of Class 47/0 members were originally fitted with steam heat, using the Stones OK4610, or Spanner Mk 111 steam generator; however, the majority have either been removed or isolated.
6. Locomotives 47401-47420 have a Tractive Effort of 55,000lb (245kN).
7. Brush TG160-16 ETS generators are fitted to Nos 47401-47420.
8. Brush BL100-30 ETS alternators are fitted to Nos 47421-47665.
9. Locomotives Nos 47401-47550/553-649 are fitted with standard 745gal (3,477lit) tanks, while Nos 47551/552/650-665 are fitted with 1,296gal (5,892lit) tanks.
10. Some members of Class 47/4 are fitted with dual steam and electric heat equipment, but the steam facility is being progressively removed.
11. The maximum speed of the Class 47/0 and 47/3 locomotives was reduced to 75mph from mid-1987 to improve reliability.

## Subclass variations

Class 47/0: This classification includes locomotives numbered in the 47/1 and 47/2 series, and covers locomotives built with steam heat equipment, although most are now isolated.

Class 47/3: Locomotives built without train heating facilities, primarily for freight train operation.

Class 47/4: This classification now includes locomotives in the number ranges 47/5 and 47/6, which are fitted for electric or dual heat operation.

Class 47/7: The 16 Class 47/7s are similar to Class 47/4s but are fitted with remote control equipment permitting them to operate at the remote ends of trains formed with a DBSO leading.

Class 47/9: This sub-Class consists of only one locomotive, which was converted as an active test bed for new equipment used in the Class 58 build.

Below:
*Various body modifications exist within the substantial Class 47 fleet. The drawing here represents a standard Class 47/0 locomotive, retaining the steam heating boiler water tanks on the underframe. Reference to the illustrations will show detail differences in the various sub-classes.*

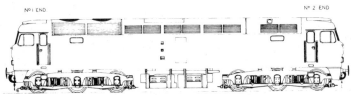

Above:

*Class 47 cab layout: 1. Train brake valve, 2. Locomotive brake valve, 3. Headlight switch,
4. Main reservoir gauge, 5. Bogie brake cylinder gauge, 6. Vacuum gauge,
7. Speedometer, 8. Brake pipe gauge, 9. Ampmeter, 10. Engine stopped warning light,
11. Wheelslip warning light, 12. General fault light, 13. AWS reset button, 14. Horn valve,
15. Engine start button, 16. Engine stop button, 17. Power controller, 18. Master switch,
19. Master key socket, 20. Train heat 'on' warning light, 21. Overload reset button,
22. Fire alarm test button, 23. Heat indicator dimmer switch, 24. Compartment light
switch, 25. Foot warmer switch, 26. Cab heat switch driver's side, 27. Cab heat switch
driver's assistant's side, 28. Tail light switch, 29. Demister switch, 30. Desk light switch,
31. Marker light switch, 32. ETS 'on' button, 33. ETS 'off' button, 34. AWS indicator.*
Colin J. Marsden

Below:

*The basic Class 47 locomotive is the Class 47/0, originally fitted with steam heat
equipment, which has now been largely isolated. Both sides of the locomotive body are
the same, but the grille and louvre arrangement differs at both ends. With No 2 end
nearest, Class 47/0 No 47032 is illustrated. Main compartments are: A. No 2 end, B. No 1
end, 1. Boiler compartment, 2. Electric control equipment, 3. Generator group, 4. Power
unit, 5. Radiator group, 6. Air compressor and pump set, 7. Battery box, 8. Boiler water
tank (removed on many locomotives), 9. Hydrostatic fan, 10. Removable roof sections.*
Colin J. Marsden

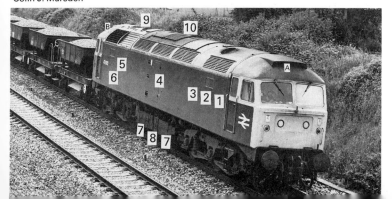

*Class 47 front end layouts: 1. Front marker lights, 2. Red 'tail' indicators, 3. High intensity headlight, 4. Main reservoir pipe, 5. Vacuum pipe, 6. Coupling, 7. Air brake pipe, 8. ETS socket, 9. ETS jumper, 10. Steam pipe (fitted to some Class 47/0 locomotives, and a few Class 47/4s), 11. Train lighting push-pull RCH jumpers.*
Colin J. Marsden (4), Michael J. Collins (1)

**Below:**

*The Class 47/3 sub-class consists of a fleet of 81 locomotives that were not given the facility to provide train heat of any type and were thus designated for freight use only. Their external appearance is the same as that of the Class 47/0, and on some examples the underslung boiler water tank has been removed and replaced by a space frame. The upper illustration shows No 47312 from the No 1 end, while the lower plate shows No 47361* Wilton Endeavour. *The latter locomotive sports a revised livery with wrap-around yellow ends and black window surrounds.*
Colin J. Marsden, Michael J. Collins

Below:
*The largest sub-class within the Class 47 fleet is Class 47/4 which in 1988 consisted of some 240 members. The Class 47/4s are locomotives fitted with Electric Train Supply (ETS) equipment and, in most cases, have had their former boiler water tanks removed. Apart from the addition of ETS jumpers on the front, the Class 47/4s are the same as the previously illustrated members. The upper illustration shows No 47470* University of Edinburgh, *sporting conventional blue livery, while the lower illustration shows No 47609* Fire Fly *painted in the latest InterCity colours, which are being progressively applied to IC sector locomotives.* Both: Colin J. Marsden

Top:
*A fleet of 16 Class 47/7s are operated in Scotland. These are basically an ETS locomotive, fitted additionally with train lighting wire push-pull RCH equipment to enable operation at the remote end of Edinburgh-Glasgow InterCity services. The addition of these nose end jumpers makes them easily distinguishable from other Class 47 locomotives. Other alterations effected during the conversion were the provision of a second fuel tank, located between the bogies, and the fitting of cab-to-cab communication equipment. All Class 47/7s are painted in ScotRail livery and are allocated to Eastfield depot. No 47707 Holyrood is illustrated.   Colin J. Marsden*

Above:
*Class 47/0 No 47046 suffered collision damage in the early 1970s and was rebuilt by BREL Crewe as a test bed for the then-projected Class 56 equipment, being renumbered 47601. After the Class 56 project commenced the locomotive was again rebuilt by Crewe as a test bed for Class 58 equipments and subsequently renumbered 47901. A number of minor detail differences can be found on this locomotive, the most important being that it is air braked-only. Other body alterations carried out included the plating over of one side window at No 2 end, the fitting of ventilation louvres above the cab doors, and the installation of a sanding system. No 47901 is allocated to Bristol and usually operates stone traffic in the Westbury area.   Colin J. Marsden*

Above:
*To mark the 150th anniversary of the GWR in 1985, four WR allocated Class 47/4s, Nos 47079/484/500/628, were repainted in BR Brunswick green livery, with bodyside lining. The nameplates, which were all associated with the GWR were recast into GWR style, and cast numberplates were provided. The green livery is expected to be retained on locomotives 47484/500/628 as long as they stay on WR books. No 47484 Isambard Kingdom Brunel is illustrated, with its No 1 end nearest the camera.* Colin J. Marsden

Below:
*Sector ownership of locomotives commenced in May 1987. However, prior to this a number of sector-identified locomotives were repainted into their 'new livery'. Under the 1987 sector policy InterCity owns 78 Class 47s, all of which will eventually be repainted into their colour scheme, as depicted here on No 47613* North Star *outside Old Oak Common depot.* Colin J. Marsden

Top:

*The new Railfreight Sub-Sector livery looks striking on all traction and especially suits the bodylines of the Class 47 fleet. Sporting the Railfreight Construction logo, No 47079 is illustrated. Note the cast depot crest on the cabside.* Colin J. Marsden

Above:

*The ScotRail livery is similar to the InterCity scheme, but with a blue band in place of the red. This scheme has been applied to all Class 47/7s and one Class 47/4. Other ScotRail-allocated Class 47/4s carry the normal InterCity livery, but with the legend 'ScotRail' in place of 'InterCity'. ScotRail No 47642 is seen here at Waterloo.* Colin J. Marsden

Above:
*Five Class 47/4 locomotives are allocated to Network SouthEast, being allocated to Stratford and Old Oak Common. In 1987 no fewer than six locomotives had been outshopped in NSE livery! No 47581 Great Eastern is seen inside the Diesel Repair Shop (DRS) at Stratford in February 1987.* Colin J. Marsden

Below:
*To increase their operational range, Class 47s Nos 47551-552/650-665 have each been fitted with an additional fuel tank which increases the capacity to 1,295gal and is situated around the battery box at the No 2 end of the locomotive, the position of which is marked on this illustration of No 47656 by the letter 'X'.* Colin J. Marsden

# Class 50

| Sub-Class | 50/0 | 50/1 |
|---|---|---|
| Former Class code: | 27/3 | — |
| Number range: | 50001-50050 | 50149 |
| Former number range: | D400-D449 | 50049 |
| Built by: | EE (Vulcan Foundry) Ltd | Rebuilt Laira |
| Introduced: | 1967-68 | Orig 1968, Rebuilt 1987 |
| Wheel arrangement: | Co-Co | Co-Co |
| Weight (operational): | 117 tonnes | 117 tonnes |
| Height: | 12ft 10¾in (3.95m) | 12ft 10¾in (3.95m) |
| Width: | 9ft 1¼in (2.77m) | 9ft 1¼in (2.17m) |
| Length: | 68ft 6in (20.87m) | 68ft 6in (20.87m) |
| Minimum curve negotiable: | 4 chains (80.46m) | 4 chains (80.46m) |
| Maximum speed: | 100mph (161km/h) | 80mph (129km/h) |
| Wheelbase: | 56ft 2in (17.11m) | 56ft 2in (17.11m) |
| Bogie wheelbase: | 13ft 6in (4.11m) | 13ft 6in (4.11m) |
| Bogie pivot centres: | 42ft 8in (13.00m) | 42ft 8in (13.00m) |
| Wheel diameter (driving): | 3ft 7in (1.09m) | 3ft 7in (1.09m) |
| Brake type: | Dual | Dual |
| Sanding equipment: | Not fitted | Not fitted |
| Heating type: | Electric — Index 61 | Not available |
| Route availability: | 6 | 6 |
| Multiple coupling restriction: | Orange Square | Orange Square |
| Brake force: | 59 tonnes | 59 tonnes |
| Engine type: | English Electric 16CSVT | English Electric 16CSVT |
| Engine horsepower: | 2,700hp (2,014kW) | 2,450hp |
| Power at rail: | 2,070hp (1,540kW) | 1,890hp |
| Tractive effort: | 48,500lb (216kN) | 48,500lb (216kN) |
| Cylinder bore: | 10in (0.25m) | 10in (0.25m) |
| Cylinder stroke: | 12in (0.30m) | 12in (0.30m) |
| Main generator type: | EE840-4B | EE840-4B |
| Auxiliary generator type: | EE911-5C | EE911-5C |
| ETS generator type: | EE915-1B | EE915-1B |
| Number of traction motors: | 6 | 6 |
| Traction motor type: | EE538-5A | EE538-1A |
| Gear ratio: | 53 : 18 | 53 : 18 |
| Fuel tank capacity: | 1,055gal (4,797lit) | 1,055gal (4,797lit) |
| Cooling water capacity: | 280gal (1,272lit) | 280gal (1,272lit) |
| Lubricating oil capacity: | 130gal (591lit) | 130gal (591lit) |
| Region of allocation: | Western | Western |
| Sector ownership: | D, N, R | F |

Right:
*This drawing is representative of the complete fleet and shows a locomotive in refurbished condition with plated roof section above side air louvres, nose end fixed beam headlight and plated over sandboxes.*

Far right:
*Today 26 members of the 45-strong Class 50 fleet are operated by Network SouthEast (NSE), being allocated to Old Oak Common and Plymouth. Most NSE Class 50s display the distinctive blue, white, red and grey livery which is seen here on No 50002* Superb *outside Old Oak Common depot.* Colin J. Marsden

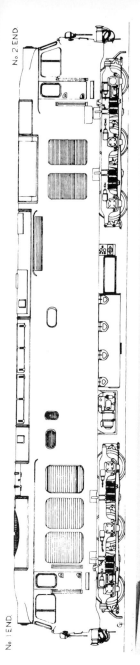

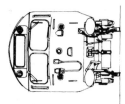

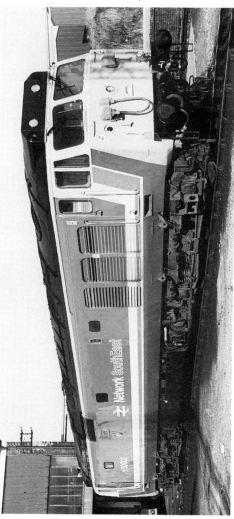

Below:

*One of the most popular classes of diesel locomotive is the Class 50s, allocated to the WR, and operating on the WR, parts of the SR, as well as inter-regional duties as far north as Birmingham. The two different body sides are shown in these two illustrations. The upper plate shows No 50033 from No 1 end driver's side, while the lower plate of No 50036, also from the No 1 end, is taken from the driver's assistant's side. Main equipment areas are: 1. Radiator compartment, 2. Air compressor, 3. Fuel tank, 4. Battery box, 5. Engine compartment, 6. Generator compartment, 7. Brake equipment, 8. Control cubicle.   Colin J. Marsden*

Right:

*Following the introduction of sector ownership, the Class 50s have been operated by Network SouthEast (29), Provincial Services (6), Parcels (9) and Departmental (2). The NSE operated locomotives are mostly painted in its distinctive livery, displayed here on No 50019* Ramillies *outside Doncaster Works. Note that the nameplate position is different on NSE liveried locomotives.   Colin J. Marsden*

Above:

*Class 50 cab-layout. 1. Locomotive brake valve, 2. Train brake valve, 3. Brake pipe pressure gauge, 4. Vacuum gauge, 5. Bogie brake cylinder pressure gauge, 6. AWS re-set button, 7. AWS indicator, 8. Wheelslip brake button, 9. Windscreen wiper valve, 10. Windscreen washer button, 11. Indicator dimmer switch, 12. Horn valve, 13. Speedometer, 14. Wheelslip warning light, 15. Overload re-set button, 16. Engine start button, 17. Pre-select tractive effort switch, 18. Traction ammeter, 19. Master switch, 20, Power controller, 21, Engine stop button, 22. Fault indicator, 23. Engine stopped warning light, 24. Fire alarm test button, 25. Slow speed speedometer, 26. Slow speed setting switch, 27. Main reservoir gauge, 28. Cab ventilation control, 29. Cab cooker switch, 30. Cab cooker/hotplate, 31. Electric train supply warning light, 32. ETS light dimmer switch, 33. ETS 'on' button, 34. ETS 'off' button. Cab illustrated is for unrefurbished locomotive.* Colin J. Marsden

Below:
*Class 50 front end layout. 1. Front marker light, 2. Windscreen washer jet, 3. Red 'tail' indicator, 4. Multiple control jumper cable, 5. Multiple control jumper socket, 6. High intensity headlight, 7. ETS jumper cable, 8. ETS jumper socket, 9. Locomotive air control pipe, 10. Main reservoir pipe, 11. Vacuum pipe, 12. Coupling, 13. Air brake pipe, 14. Snowplough bracket.* Colin J. Marsden

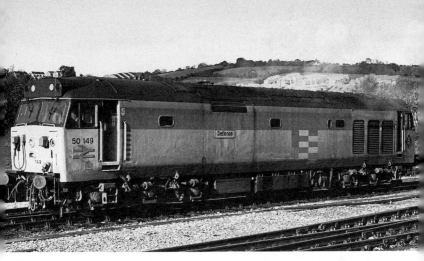

Top:
*To mark the 150th anniversary of the GWR in 1985 Class 50 No 50007* Hercules *was repainted into BR Brunswick green livery, given cast names and numberplates, and renamed* Sir Edward Elgar. *No 50007 still retains this distinctive livery, and is therefore immediately recognisable. No 50007 is seen outside Old Oak Common depot.*
Colin J. Marsden

Above:
*In the autumn of 1987 Laira Depot modified No 50049 to a Railfreight Sector specification by re-gearing for 80mph working. The locomotive, modified as experiment DL915, emerged as No 50149 in the new Railfreight Sub-Sector livery and undertook a series of trials at the end of 1987. By early 1988 the decision was taken not to persist with this experiment and No 50149 was deployed on Cornish freight duties. The locomotive is illustrated at Exeter.* Colin J. Marsden

# Class 56

| | |
|---|---|
| **Number range:** | 56001-56135 |
| **Built by:** | Electroputere in Romania, BREL Doncaster and Crewe |
| **Introduced:** | 1976-84 |
| **Wheel arrangement:** | Co-Co |
| **Weight (operational):** | 126 tonnes |
| **Height:** | 13ft 0in (3.96m) |
| **Width:** | 9ft 2in (2.79m) |
| **Length:** | 63ft 6in (19.39m) |
| **Minimum curve negotiable:** | 4 chains (80.46m) |
| **Maximum speed:** | 80mph (129km/h) |
| **Wheelbase:** | 47ft 10in (14.58m) |
| **Bogie wheelbase:** | 13ft 5⅞in (4.10m) |
| **Bogie pivot centres:** | 37ft 8in (11.48m) |
| **Wheel diameter (driving):** | 3ft 9in (1.14m) |
| **Brake type:** | Air |
| **Sanding equipment:** | Pneumatic |
| **Heating type:** | Not fitted |
| **Route availability:** | 7 |
| **Multiple coupling restriction:** | Red Diamond |
| **Brake force:** | 60 tonnes |
| **Engine type:** | Ruston-Paxman 16RK3CT |
| **Engine horsepower:** | 3,250hp (2,420kW) |
| **Power at rail:** | 2,400hp (1,790kW) |
| **Tractive effort:** | 61,800lb (277kN) |
| **Cylinder bore:** | 10in (0.25m) |
| **Cylinder stroke:** | 12in (0.30m) |
| **Main alternator type:** | Brush BA1101A |
| **Auxiliary alternator type:** | Brush BAA602A |
| **Number of traction motors:** | 6 |
| **Traction motor type:** | Brush TMH73-62 |
| **Gear ratio:** | 63 : 16 |
| **Fuel tank capacity:** | 1,150gal (5,228lit) |
| **Cooling water capacity:** | 308gal (1,400lit) |
| **Lubricating oil capacity:** | 120gal (545lit) |
| **Regions of allocation:** | Midland, Western |
| **Sector ownership:** | F |

## Major detail variations

No 56042 is mounted on CP1 bogies.

Nos 56073/74 are fitted with remote control equipment, and have roof mounted warning beacons.

Nos 56001-055 were built with small horn grilles on the ends, lipped buffer beams and inset marker lights.

Nos 56056-135 were built with larger horn grilles, protruding marker lights and a body-mounted step in place of the lipped buffer beam.

Locomotive/shore telephones are progressively being fitted giving a small roof-mounted aerial.

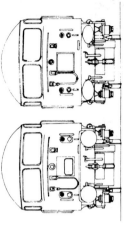

N° 1 END.

N° 2 END

Above:
Various detail differences exist within the Class 56 fleet, mainly involving front end arrangement and cab window detail. Both body sides are identical. Two front ends are shown — on the left is the original design applied to Nos 56001-055, and on the right is the front detail on Nos 56056-135. Some of the early designed locomotives may be outshopped with the later cab arrangement following collision damage repairs. Round or oval buffers are carried on either front end.

Above:

*Britain's first purpose-built Railfreight locomotives were the Class 56s, which commenced entry into service in 1977. Today a total of 135 are in service, and several detail differences exist within the fleet. The first 30 locomotives were built under contract in Romania, and are distinguishable from British-built examples by having the two cabside windows as individual units, with the front mounted in a rubber grommet, whereas on British-built locomotives the cabside windows are mounted in a common frame with a dividing column. Door windows on Romanian locomotives are also grommet-mounted, whereas British examples use an aluminium frame to hold the window. These two illustrations show a Romanian example (upper), and a British example (lower). Main equipment areas are: 1. Electrical control cubicle, 2. Alternator compartment, 3. Power unit compartment, 4. Radiator compartment, 5. Air compressor, 6. Battery box, 7. Fuel tank, 8. Sand box.   Michael J. Collins, Graham Scott-Lowe*

Above:

*Class 56 cab layout: 1. Train brake valve, 2. Locomotive brake valve, 3. Emergency brake plunger, 4. Horn valve, 5. AWS reset button, 6. Power controller, 7. Master switch (OFF/REV/EO/FOR), 8. Driver-guard communication handset, 9. Demister switch, 10 Headlight switch, 11. Cab heat switch, 12. AWS indicator, 13. Windscreen wiper control, 14. Parking brake indicator, 15. Parking brake 'on' button, 16. Parking brake 'off' button, 17. Main reservoir gauge, 18. Brake overcharge button, 19. Fire alarm test button, 20. Brake cylinder pressure gauge, 21. Brake pipe gauge, 22. Speedometer, 23. AWS warning indicator, 24. Engine stopped indicator, 25. Wheelslip indicator, 26. Fault light, 27. Slow speed control speedometer, 28. Ampmeter, 29. Slow speed control switch, 30. Buzzer, 31. Engine start button, 32. Engine stop button, 33, Compartment light switch, 34. Tail light switch (left), 35. Tail light switch (right), 36. Front marker light switch, 37. Driver's key position.* Colin J. Marsden

Below:

*The Class 56 locomotives were built in various batches, therefore a number of minor differences exist, particularly with the front end. Locomotives Nos 56001-055 were built with a small horn grille, top buffer beam lip, and inset marker/tail lights, whereas subsequent locomotives were given a large horn grille, had no buffer beam lip, and the marker/tail lights were fitted on to the bodywork. Nos 56001-055 were also built with smaller headlights. No 56058 is illustrated from No 1 end.* Colin J. Marsden

Below:
*Class 56 front end layout. Although this illustration is of one of the earlier design, the equipment layout is applicable for all Class 56 front ends. 1. High intensity headlight, 2. Horn grille, 3. Red 'tail' indicator, 4. Marker light, 5. Multiple control jumper cable, 6. Multiple control jumper socket, 7. Coupling, 8. Main reservoir pipe, 9. Air brake pipe.*
Michael J. Collins

Above:
*Locomotives Nos 56001-083 were outshopped in standard BR blue. After this a revised livery was applied. Showing the original blue livery, No 56062 passes Ilkeston with a southbound MGR coal train.* Colin J. Marsden

Below:
*Locomotives Nos 56085-135 were built in blue livery with wrap-around yellow warning ends, together with black cab window surrounds and grey roofs. This livery is displayed on Crewe-built No 56130.* Colin J. Marsden

Top:
*Following the introduction of sector liveries the Class 56s started to emerge in Railfreight grey, with wrap-around yellow ends, black window surrounds, and small numerals. From May 1987 the Railfreight livery was further revised with a red band being applied to the bottom of the body, extending completely round the locomotive. No 56007 is illustrated in original Railfreight livery.* Colin J. Marsden

Above:
*Locomotive No 56042 was selected during construction to be fitted with CP1 bogies, a prototype design of a bogie later installed under the Class 58s. The locomotive still retains these unique bogies, and is immediately recognisable from other locomotives. It is understood that although the experiment with this bogie design is now complete, it is not possible to replace them with the conventional type. No 56042 is seen at BREL Doncaster Works.* Colin J. Marsden

Above:
*Locomotives Nos 56073/074 were built with a remote slow speed control device. This included the installation of orange flashing beacons on the roof to warn staff that the locomotives were under remote control. Although it is unlikely that this equipment will ever be used again, the flashing beacon lights are retained. No 56074* Kellingley Colliery *is illustrated.* Colin J. Marsden

Below:
*All Class 56s are operated by the Railfreight sector, and allocated to the Midland and Western Regions. Using all its 3,250hp, No 56033 pulls a heavy ARC stone train off the Frome line at Clink Road Junction in March 1986.* Colin J. Marsden

# Class 58

| | |
|---|---|
| **Number range:** | 58001-58050 |
| **Built by:** | BREL Doncaster |
| **Introduced:** | 1983-87 |
| **Wheel arrangement:** | Co-Co |
| **Weight (operational):** | 130 tonnes |
| **Height:** | 12ft 10in (3.91m) |
| **Width:** | 8ft 10½in (2.70m) |
| **Length:** | 62ft 9½in (19.13m) |
| **Minimum curve negotiable:** | 4 chains (80.46m) |
| **Maximum speed:** | 80mph (129km/h) |
| **Wheelbase:** | 48ft 9in (14.85m) |
| **Bogie wheelbase:** | 13ft 8½in (4.18m) |
| **Bogie pivot centres:** | 35ft 5½in (10.80m) |
| **Wheel diameter (driving):** | 3ft 8in (1.12m) |
| **Brake type:** | Air |
| **Sanding equipment:** | Pneumatic |
| **Heating type:** | Not fitted |
| **Route availability:** | 7 |
| **Multiple coupling restriction:** | Red Diamond |
| **Brake force:** | 62 tonnes |
| **Engine type:** | Ruston-Paxman 12RK3ACT |
| **Engine horsepower:** | 3,300hp (2,460kW) |
| **Power at rail:** | 2,387hp (1,780kW) |
| **Tractive effort:** | 61,800lb (275kN) |
| **Cylinder bore:** | 10in (0.25m) |
| **Cylinder stroke:** | 12in (0.30m) |
| **Main generator type:** | Brush BA1101B |
| **Auxiliary generator type:** | Brush BAA602B |
| **Number of traction motors:** | 6 |
| **Traction motor type:** | Brush TM73-62 |
| **Gear ratio:** | 63 : 16 |
| **Fuel tank capacity:** | 985gal (4,480lit) |
| **Cooling water capacity:** | 264gal (1,200lit) |
| **Lubricating oil capacity:** | 110gal (416lit) |
| **Region of allocation:** | Midland |
| **Sector ownership:** | F |

No 58050 is fitted with 'Sepex' modified traction equipment.

Right:
*This is the latest BR designed diesel locomotive. They are of modular construction, each major component being fitted to a rigid frame. No significant detail differences exist amongst the locomotives in traffic. Both body sides are of identical layout.*

Far right:
*The first Class 58 to emerge in new Sub-Sector 'double grey' colours was No 58050 (the SEPEX locomotive) in October 1987, followed by all repainted examples for spring 1988. Sporting the Coal Sub-Sector colours, No 58050 is illustrated at the livery launch at Ripple Lane.* Colin J. Marsden

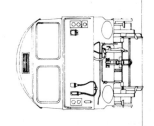

N° 2 END

N° 1 END

Above:

*Class 58 cab layout: 1. Train brake controller, 2. Locomotive brake controller, 3. Horn valve, 4. Emergency brake plunger, 5. Parking brake 'on' button, 6. Parking brake indicator, 7. Parking brake 'off' button, 8. Brake overcharge release button, 9. Brake test light, 10. AWS in/out indicator, 11. Engine stopped indicator, 12. AWS horn, 13. Wheelslip warning light, 14. Fault warning light, 15. Main reservoir gauge, 16. Brake cylinder pressure gauge, 17. Brake pipe gauge, 18. AWS indicator, 19. Speedometer, 20. Slow speed control switch, 21. Screen wash/wipe driver's side, 22. Slow speed speedometer, 23. Ammeter, 24. Engine start button, 25. Engine stop button, 26. Fire alarm test button, 27. Crew communication button, 28. Crew communication buzzer, 29. Fire bottle push-button, 30. Telephone, 31. Hotplate control, 32. Screen wash/wipe driver's assistant's side, 33. Cab heat switch, 34. Cab temperature control, 35. Master switch (OFF/REV/EO/FOR), 36. Power controller, 37. AWS reset button.* Colin J. Marsden

Below:

*Following the Class 56 build came the Class 58 heavy freight design, differing completely from the Class 56 in that modular construction was adopted. This view shows locomotive No 58006 from the No 2 end, the main areas of equipment being: 1. Cab module, 2. Clean air compartment, rectifier unit, control cubicle and alternator, 3. Power unit compartment, 4. Radiator compartment, 5. Battery box, 6. Main frame, with external conduit, 7. Brake equipment, 8. Air reservoir.* Colin J. Marsden

Below:
*Class 58 front end layout: 1. Red 'tail' indicator, 2. Marker light, 3. High intensity headlamp, 4. Multiple control jumper cable, 5. Multiple control jumper receptacle, 6. Coupling, 7. Engine control air pipe, 8. Main reservoir pipe, 9. Brake pipe.*
Colin J. Marsden

Above:
*These two illustrations are both taken with the locomotive's No 1 end on the left, main bodyside equipment items are the same as on the previous side illustration, the only significant difference being the battery isolating switch on the right adjacent to the battery box. If these two illustrations are compared a noticeable modification is apparent, namely the installation of inspection door handles, which commenced with locomotive No 58015. This modification was carried out due to maintenance problems. The above illustration shows No 58003, while the lower plate shows No 58021.*
Both: Colin J. Marsden

Displaying the conventional all blue livery with yellow/black wasp ends is No 08562. This dual-braked example also carries the name The Doncaster Postman.
Colin J. Marsden

# Class 59

| | |
|---|---|
| **Number range:** | 59001-59004 |
| **Model:** | JT26SS-55 |
| **Built by:** | General Motors Ltd, Illinois, USA |
| **Introduced:** | 1986 |
| **Wheel arrangement:** | Co-Co |
| **Weight (operational):** | 126 tonnes |
| **Height:** | 12ft 10in (3.91m) |
| **Width:** | 8ft 8¼in (2.65m) |
| **Length:** | 70ft 0½in (21.40m) |
| **Minimum curve negotiable:** | |
| **Maximum speed:** | 60mph (97km/h) |
| **Wheelbase:** | 56ft 9in (17.29m) |
| **Bogie wheelbase:** | 13ft 7in (4.14m) |
| **Bogie pivot centres:** | 43ft 6in (13.25m) |
| **Wheel diameter (driving):** | 3ft 6in (1.06m) |
| **Brake type:** | Air |
| **Sanding equipment:** | Pneumatic |
| **Heating type:** | Not fitted |
| **Route availability:** | 7 |
| **Multiple coupling restriction:** | Within type only |
| **Brake force:** | 69 tonnes |
| **Engine type:** | EMD 645E3C |
| **Engine horsepower:** | 3,000hp (2,238kW) |
| **Power at rail:** | |
| **Tractive effort:** | 122,000lb (573kN) |
| **Cylinder bore:** | 9¹/₁₆in (0.23m) |
| **Cylinder stroke:** | 10in (0.25m) |
| **Traction alternator type:** | EMD AR11 MLD D14A |
| **Number of traction motors:** | 6 |
| **Traction motor type:** | EMD D77B |
| **Gear ratio:** | |
| **Fuel tank capacity:** | 919gal (4,543lit) |
| **Cooling water capacity:** | 212gal (962lit) |
| **Lubricating oil capacity:** | 202gal (920lit) |
| **Owner and operator:** | Foster Yeoman Ltd, Merehead |

These locomotives are operated by BR Railfreight Sector, on behalf of Foster Yeoman Ltd.

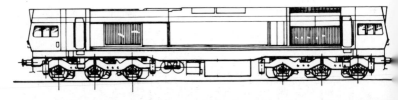

Above:

*Class 59 cab layout: 1. AWS reset button, 2. Sand control lever, 3. Train brake controller, 4. Locomotive brake controller, 5. Normal/no sand control switch, 6. Sand cut-out indicator, 7. Emergency brake plunger, 8. Horn valve, 9. Parking brake 'on' button, 10. Parking brake indicator, 11. Parking brake 'off' button, 12. Brake overcharge button, 13. Main reservoir gauge, 14. Bogie brake cylinder gauge, 15. Brake test indicator, 16. AWS in/out indicator, 17. Engine stopped indicator, 18. Brake pipe gauge, 19. AWS buzzer, 20. AWS indicator, 21. Wheelslip indicator, 22. General fault indicator, 23. Speedometer, 24. Indicator dimmer switch, 25. Screen wash/wipe (driver's side), 26. Ampmeter, 27. Fire alarm test button, 28. Engine prime button, 29. Engine start button, 30. Engine stop button, 31. Crew communication buzzer — alarm, 32. Crew communication buzzer — button, 33. Fire bottle push button, 34. Hot plate switch, 35. Power controller, 36. Master switch (removable handle), 37. Crew communication handset.* Colin J. Marsden

Below:

*When the naming ceremony was carried out at Merehead, a brass bell was presented to Foster Yeoman which is now fixed on the front of the No 1 end of No 59001, thus affording immediate recognition of this locomotive. No 59001 is illustrated at the Merehead depot.* Stephen Montgomery

From mid-1983 a number of Class 20s were outshopped in the Railfreight Sector grey livery, complete with wrap-round yellow ends, black window surrounds and red solebar. This livery is displayed on No 20090 at Derby Works. Colin J. Marsden

After the standard Railfreight grey had been applied to a number of Class 31/1s, a modification incorporating a red solebar was introduced. No 31268 is illustrated from the No 2 end whilst on display at Basingstoke.   Colin J. Marsden

Below:
*Class 59 front end layout: 1. Red 'tail' marker light, 2. Marker light, 3. High-intensity headlight, 4. Multiple control jumper socket, cable kept inside locomotive, 5. Coupling, 6. Brake pipe, 7. Main reservoir pipe, 8. Horns (behind grille).* Colin J. Marsden

Right:
*The four Class 59 machines are the first privately-owned diesel locomotives operating on BR tracks, they are owned by Foster Yeoman, and are only scheduled to operate that company's stone traffic from the Foster Yeoman stone terminal at Merehead, where the locomotives are allocated. These illustrations show the two different sides of the locomotive, both taken from the No 1 end. The main equipment areas being marked. 1. Exhaust silencer group (removable hatch), 2. Power unit/alternator compartment, 3. Cooling system air intakes, 4. Cooling system air outlet, 5. Sand boxes, 6. Battery box, 7. Fuel tank, 7. Internal air filtration group, 9. Engine access hatch.*
Both: Colin J. Marsden

At the time of writing all remaining Class 33s are painted in the conventional rail blue livery with the exception of No 33008 which is in Brunswick green. No 33001 passes the village of Basing on 23 April 1987 with the 10.22 Bevois Park-Halling cement.
Colin J. Marsden

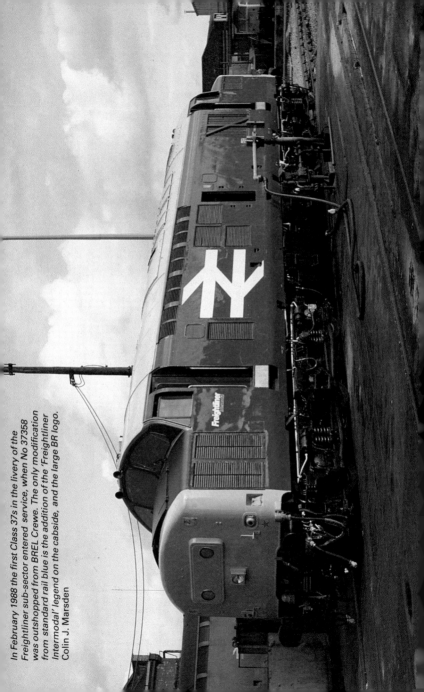

In February 1988 the first Class 37s in the livery of the Freightliner sub-sector entered service, when No 37358 was outshopped from BREL Crewe. The only modification from standard rail blue is the addition of the 'Freightliner Intermodal' legend on the cabside, and the large BR logo. Colin J. Marsden

# Class 73

| Class: | 73/0 | 73/1 |
|---|---|---|
| Former Class codes: | 72 | — |
| SR Class Code: | JA | JB |
| Number range: | 73001-73006 | 73101-73141/201-212 |
| Former number range: | E6001-E6006 | E6007-E6049 |
| Built by: | BR Eastleigh | EE Ltd |
| Introduced: | 1962 | 1965-67 |
| Wheel arrangement: | Bo-Bo | Bo-Bo |
| Weight (operational): | 76 tonnes | 77 tonnes |
| Height: | 12ft 6⅛in (3.81m) | 12ft 6⅛in (3.81m) |
| Width: | 8ft 8in (2.64m) | 8ft 8in (2.64m) |
| Length (buffers extended): | 55ft 8in (16.96m) | 55ft 8in (16.96m) |
| (buffers retracted): | 52ft 6in (16.00m) | 52ft 6in (16.00m) |
| Minimum curve negotiable: | 4 chains | 4 chains |
| Maximum speed: | 80mph (129km/h) | 90mph (145km/h) |
| Wheelbase: | 40ft 9in (12.42m) | 40ft 9in (12.42m) |
| Bogie wheelbase: | 8ft 9in (2.66m) | 8ft 9in (2.66m) |
| Bogie pivot centres: | 32ft 0in (11.27m) | 32ft 0in (11.27m) |
| Wheel diameter: | 3ft 4in (1.01m) | 3ft 4in (1.01m) |
| Brake type: | Dual, EP | Dual, EP |
| Sanding equipment: | Pneumatic | Pneumatic |
| Heating type: | Electric — Index 66[1] | Electric — Index 66[1] |
| Route availability: | 6 | 6 |
| Coupling restriction: | Blue Star[2] | Blue Star[2] |
| Brake force: | 31 tonnes | 31 tonnes |
| Nominal supply voltage: | 600-750V dc | 600-750V dc |
| Engine type: | EE 4SRKT Mk II | EE 4SRKT Mk II |
| Engine horsepower (electric): | 1,420hp | 1,420hp |
| (diesel): | 600hp | 600hp |
| Tractive effort (electric): | 42,000lb (187kN) | 40,000lb (179kN) |
| (diesel): | 34,000lb (152kN) | 36,000lb (160kN) |
| Cylinder bore: | 10in (0.25m) | 10in (0.25m) |
| Cylinder stroke: | 12in (0.30m) | 12in (0.30m) |
| Main generator type: | EE824-3D | EE824-5D |

| | | |
|---|---|---|
| **Auxiliary generator type:** | EE908-3C | EE908-5C |
| **Traction motor type:** | EE542A | EE546-1B |
| **Gear ratio:** | 62 : 17 | 62 : 17 |
| **Fuel tank capacity:** | 340gal (1,546lit) | 310gal (1,409lit) |
| **Cooling water capacity:** | — | — |
| **Region of allocation:** | Southern | Southern |
| **Sector ownership:** | D, N, R | D, F, I, N, R |

*Notes:*

[1] ETS is only available under electric conditions. A preheat system is available on the Class 73/0s.

[2] Multiple coupling conforms to Blue Star for diesel operation; in addition each sub-class can operate in multiple together, and in multiple with Class 33/1 locomotives, as well as selected post-1951 EMU stock using the 27-wire waist height jumper connections.

[3] Locomotives 73201-212 are dedicated to the InterCity Victoria-Gatwick service.

## Subclass variations

Class 73/0: The prototype Electro-Diesel locomotive fleet, constructed by BR at Eastleigh. The design proved suitable for SR operation, and the production fleet was ordered. The 73/0 fleet have an additional jumper cable on the nose end, and grille differences on the body sides.

Class 73/1: The production fleet of Electro-Diesel locomotives, constructed by English Electric. They are mounted on a revised bogie design, and have side grille differences to the Class 73/0.

Class 73/2: This new sub-class introduced in spring 1988 is for locomotives used exclusively on Gatwick Express duties.

Today the Class 73/1s are largely outshopped in InterCity colours, while the Class 73/0s sport the 'More-Yellow' colours.

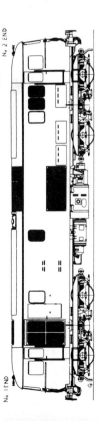

Left:
*Three sub-classes of Class 73 are in service. This drawing is of the original Class 73/0 design.*

No I END

No 2 END

The InterCity Sector own a significant number of Class 47/4 locomotives and their distinctive livery is progressively being applied. Old Oak Common-allocated No 47612 is illustrated on the Old Oak Common turntable on 11 April 1987. Colin J. Marsden

To commemorate the 150th anniversary of the Great Western Railway several WR-allocated locomotives were repainted in mock GWR green livery. One example was Class 50 No 50007 Sir Edward Elgar, shown in this illustration at Westbury.

Colin J. Marsden

Above:
*Class 73 cab layout, this illustration is of the driver's side of a Class 73/1. 1. Locomotive brake valve, 2. Train brake valve, 3. Sanding button, 4. Exhauster high speed button, 5. Brake selector switch, 6. AWS indicator, 7. Windscreen wiper valve, 8. Horn valve, 9. Shoe down button, 10. Anti-slip brake button, 11. Rear cab horn button, 12. AWS reset button, 13. Driver's key socket, 14. Master switch, 15. Diesel power controller, 16. Electric power controller, 17. Brake/main reservoir pipe gauge, 18. Brake cylinder gauge, 19. Vacuum gauge, 20. Resistance indicator, 21. Line indicator, 22. Engine running indicator, 23. Auxiliary power indicator, 24. Wheel slip indicator, 25. Earth fault indicator, 26. Speedometer, 27. Engine stop switch, 28. Auto engine start switch, 29. Demister switch, 30. Route indicator light switch, 31. Instrument light switch.*
Colin J. Marsden

Below:

*The six Class 73/0 locomotives were the prototype Class 73s built during the early 1960s in an experiment with the dual power concept — the locomotive having its own diesel engine at one end. The two sides of the locomotive are different, as the positions of air louvres and windows are revised. All six locomotives are allocated to Stewarts Lane and with the exception of No 73004 which is in Bluebell blue are painted in the 'more-yellow' livery as displayed here on No 73001, with its electric end nearest the camera. If this and the illustrations of the Class 73/1s are compared the detail differences are quite obvious.* Brian Morrison

Left:

*Class 73 front end layout (left) Class 73/0, (right) Class 73/1. 1. Multiple unit control jumper, 2. Waist height brake pipe, 3. Waist height main reservoir pipe, 4. Multiple unit control jumper receptacle, 5. Additional waist height control jumper and receptacle (Class 73/0 only), 6. Rubbing plate, 7. Engine control air pipe, 8. ETS socket, 9. Main reservoir pipe, 10. Blue star control jumper receptacle (jumper stowed inside locomotive), 11. Brake pipe, 12. Vacuum pipe, 13. Buck-eye coupling, 14. Coupling hook, 15. ETS jumper.* Both: Colin J. Marsden

In October 1987 when the Railfreight business was re-launched and the Sector was broken up into smaller sub-sectors, a new image was launched, which included the progressive application of a new double-grey livery with sector embellishments. Class 56 No 56001 displays the new double-grey livery together with the Railfreight Construction sub-sector logo. Colin J. Marsden

When constructed, all Class 58s were outshopped in Railfreight grey livery with wrap-round yellow ends, black window surrounds and red solebar. However, the new sub-sector double-grey livery will soon be applied to all outshopped examples. Displaying the original livery colours, No 58003 is illustrated at Westbury.
Colin J. Marsden

Below:

*The Class 73/1s are almost identical to the prototypes except for some slight revision to side window and louvre arrangements. This is best appreciated if the two relevant side illustrations are compared. Both show the Class 73/1 from No 2 end — main areas of equipment are marked. 1. Bogie arc guard, 2. 3rd rail collector shoe, 3. Speedometer bogie equipment, 4. Sand box, 5. Fuel tank, 6. Vacuum exhauster, 7. Diesel end of locomotive, containing power unit, generator, and coolant group, 8. Electric end of locomotive, 9. Starting resistance grille. The top illustration is of No 73112 at Stewarts Lane, and the lower of No 73108 passing Woking with an up van train. Both are painted in the InterCity livery. Both: Colin J. Marsden*

Above:
*Class 73 bogie detail. The Class 73/0 and Class 73/1 locomotives are mounted on different designs of bogie, although the basic items of equipment are similar. 1. Brake Cylinder, 2. Sand box, 3. Axlebox, 4. Bogie flash guard (only on 73/1), 5. 3rd rail collector shoe, 6. Main springing, 7. Damper, 8. Locomotive body lifting point.* Colin J. Marsden

Below:
*Twelve Class 73/1s were renumbered 73201-212 in April 1988 for the InterCity Victoria-Gatwick service, technically the locomotives are identical to the Class 73101-141 fleet. No 73210 is illustrated outside Stewarts Lane depot.* Michael J. Collins

The four privately-owned Foster Yeoman Class 59s are painted in that company's corporate colours of silver-grey and mid-blue. To conform with BR's safety requirements yellow ends are applied. No 59004 Yeoman Challenger is illustrated from its No 2 end at Old Oak Common during crew training.    Colin J. Marsden

The InterCity Sector requires 12 Class 73 locomotives to operate its 'Gatwick Express' service. Because there is no need for the auxiliary diesel engine on these services, 12 locomotives have had their engines isolated and renumbered as Class 73/2. Before conversion was authorised, No 73102 Airtour Suisse is seen at Stewarts Lane depot.
Colin J. Marsden

# Class 81

| | |
|---|---|
| **Former Class code:** | AL1 |
| **Present number range:** | 81002-81019 |
| **Former number range:** | E3001-E3023, E3096-E3097 |
| **Built by:** | BRC&W Ltd |
| **Introduced:** | 1959-64 |
| **Wheel arrangement:** | Bo-Bo |
| **Weight (operational):** | 79 tonnes |
| **Height (pantograph lowered):** | 12ft 4¼in (3.76m) |
| **Width:** | 8ft 8¼in (2.65m) |
| **Length:** | 56ft 6in (17.22m) |
| **Minimum curve negotiable:** | 4 chains (80.46m) |
| **Maximum speed:** | 80mph (129km/h)* |
| **Wheelbase:** | 42ft 3in (12.87m) |
| **Bogie wheelbase:** | 10ft 9in (3.27m) |
| **Bogie pivot centres:** | 31ft 6in (9.60m) |
| **Wheel diameter:** | 4ft 0in (1.21m) |
| **Brake type:** | Dual |
| **Sanding equipment:** | Pneumatic |
| **Heating type:** | Electric — Index 66 |
| **Route availability:** | 6 |
| **Coupling restriction:** | Not multiple fitted |
| **Brake force:** | 40 tonnes |
| **Horsepower (continuous):** | 3,200hp (2,387kW) |
| **(maximum):** | 4,200hp (3,580kW) |
| **Tractive effort (maximum):** | 50,000lb (222kN) |
| **Number of traction motors:** | 4 |
| **Traction motor type:** | AEI 189 |
| **Control system:** | LT Tap Changing |
| **Gear drive:** | Alsthom Quill, single reduction |
| **Gear ratio:** | 29 : 76 |
| **Pantograph type:** | Stone-Faiveley |
| **Rectifier type:** | Mercury Arc |
| **Nominal supply voltage:** | 25kV ac |
| **Region of allocation:** | Scottish |
| **Sector ownership:** | F, I, L |

\* Until 1986 the maximum permitted speed for the Class 81 fleet was 100mph. It is understood that the speed will be returned to its former level in due course.

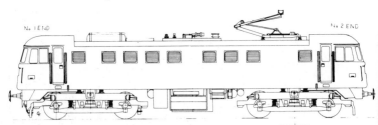

Above:
*This drawing is representative of the majority of this class. This window and ventilation arrangement on the opposite side of the body is different.*

Below:
*Class 81 cab layout. This layout is also applicable for Classes 82-85, but minor detail differences may be found. 1. Train brake valve, 2. Locomotive brake valve, 3. AWS indicator, 4. Anti-slip brake button, 5. Windscreen wiper valve, 6. Horn valve, 7. AWS reset button, 8. Windscreen washer control, 9. Pantograph up button, 10. Pantograph down button, 11. ETS 'on' button, 12. ETS 'off' button, 13. Main reservoir gauge, 14. Brake cylinder gauge, 15. Vacuum gauge, 16. Brake pipe gauge, 17. Speedometer, 18. No 1 & 2 traction motor ampmeter, 19. No 3 & 4 traction motor ampmeter, 20. Notch indicator, 21. Line indicator, 22. Fault light, 23. ETS indicator, 24. Marker light switch, 25. Instrument light switch — 1, 26. Demister switch, 27. Instrument light switch — 2, 28. Brake overcharge plunger, 29. Power controller, 30. Master switch (FOR/OFF/REV), 31. Master switch release button, 32. Master key socket, 33. Driver's safety device foot switch.    Colin J. Marsden*

Bottom:
*The Class 81s which were the pioneering class of 25kV ac electric locomotive, are now allocated to Glasgow Shields Road depot. This illustration is taken from the No 2 end of the locomotive.    Colin J. Marsden*

Although several Class 86 locomotives are owned by Network SouthEast only one, No 86401, displays their livery. The locomotive is illustrated at Basingstoke and clearly shows the front end connections including multiple control jumpers and TDM connections. Colin J. Marsden

The InterCity Sector livery is the norm for the Class 87 fleet although not all the locomotives are owned by the sector. No 87024 Lord of the Isles, which is owned by the InterCity Sector, is seen approaching Crewe on 12 February 1988. Colin J. Marsden

# Class 83

| | |
|---|---|
| **Former Class code:** | AL3 |
| **Number range (present):** | 83009-83012 |
| **Former number range:** | E3024-E3035, E3098-E3100 |
| **Built by:** | English Electric |
| **Introduced:** | 1960-62 |
| **Wheel arrangement:** | Bo-Bo |
| **Weight (operational):** | 77 tonnes |
| **Height (pantograph lowered):** | 12ft 4¼in (3.76m) |
| **Width:** | 8ft 8½in (2.65m) |
| **Length:** | 57ft 6in (17.52m) |
| **Minimum curve negotiable:** | 4 chains (80.46m) |
| **Maximum speed:** | 40mph (64km/h) |
| **Wheelbase:** | 40ft 0in (12.19m) |
| **Bogie wheelbase:** | 10ft 0in (3.04m) |
| **Bogie pivot centres:** | 30ft 0in (9.14m) |
| **Wheel diameter:** | 4ft 0in (1.21m) |
| **Brake type:** | Dual |
| **Sanding equipment:** | Pneumatic |
| **Heating type:** | Electric — Index 66 |
| **Route availability:** | 6 |
| **Coupling restriction:** | Not multiple fitted |
| **Brake force:** | 38 tonnes |
| **Horsepower (continuous):** | 2,950hp (2,200kW) |
| **(maximum):** | 4,400hp (3,280kW) |
| **Tractive effort (maximum):** | 38,000lb (169kN) |
| **Number of traction motors:** | 4 |
| **Traction motor type:** | EE 532A |
| **Control system:** | LT Tap Changing |
| **Gear drive:** | SLM flexible, single reduction |
| **Gear ratio:** | 25 : 76 |
| **Pantograph type:** | Stone-Faiveley |
| **Rectifier type:** | Mercury Arc |
| **Nominal supply voltage:** | 25kV ac |
| **Region of allocation:** | Midland |
| **Sector ownership:** | I |

The remaining Class 83s are retained at Willesden depot, for the operation of empty coaching stock trains between Willesden carriage sidings and Euston.

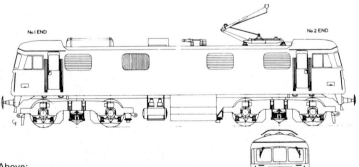

Above:
*This drawing is representative of the majority of this class. The window and ventilation arrangement on the opposite side of the body is different.*

Below:
*Class 83 is now represented by only two locomotives which are retained at Willesden for ECS operations in the London area, with a maximum permitted speed of just 40mph. These two illustrations show both sides of the locomotive design. The upper plate shows the window and grille side, while the lower illustration shows the main equipment side with four large ventilation grilles. No 83015 (now withdrawn) in the upper plate shows the locomotive from its No 2 or pantograph end, and illustrates the cross-arm pantograph. The lower plate shows No 83014 (also now withdrawn) from the grille or equipment side. No 83009 is painted in blue livery, No 83012 is in InterCity livery.* Michael J. Collins, Eric Bullen

The latest InterCity locomotive to be introduced is the Class 91 built by GEC/BREL. The locomotives, destined for the ECML electrification, are unique in BR locomotive design in having one streamlined and one slab-fronted end. Displaying the latest InterCity Swallow livery, No 91001 is illustrated at Crewe on 12 February 1988.   Colin J. Marsden

BR Research at Derby operate two locomotives for test train propulsion and experimental use. Former Class 46, No 97403 Ixion, is used for traction experiments as well as hauling test trains. The locomotive is displaying the Departmental red/blue livery inside the Vehicles Laboratory in November 1987.   Colin J. Marsden

Aabacas
Main Hoist
Aux Hoist

97403

# Class 85

| | |
|---|---|
| **Former Class code:** | AL5 |
| **Number range (present):** | 85002-83040 |
| **Former number range:** | E3056-E3095 |
| **Built by:** | BR Doncaster |
| **Introduced:** | 1961-64 |
| **Wheel arrangement:** | Bo-Bo |
| **Weight (operational):** | 83 tonnes |
| **Height (pantograph lowered):** | 12ft 4¼in (3.76m) |
| **Width:** | 8ft 8¾in (2.66m) |
| **Length:** | 56ft 5in (17.19m) |
| **Minimum curve negotiable:** | 6 chains (120.70m) |
| **Maximum speed:** | 80mph (129km/h) |
| **Wheelbase:** | 42ft 3in (12.87m) |
| **Bogie wheelbase:** | 10ft 9in (3.27m) |
| **Bogie pivot centres:** | 31ft 6in (9.60m) |
| **Wheel diameter:** | 4ft 0in (1.21m) |
| **Brake type:** | Dual |
| **Sanding equipment:** | Pneumatic |
| **Heating type:** | Electric — Index 66 |
| **Route availability:** | 6 |
| **Coupling restriction:** | Not multiple fitted |
| **Brake force:** | 41 tonnes |
| **Horsepower (continuous):** | 3,200hp (2,390kW) |
| **(maximum):** | 5,100hp (3,800kW) |
| **Tractive effort (maximum):** | 50,000lb (222kN) |
| **Number of traction motors:** | 4 |
| **Traction motor type:** | AEI 189 |
| **Control system:** | LT Tap Changing |
| **Gear drive:** | Alsthom Quill, single reduction |
| **Gear ratio:** | 29 : 76 |
| **Pantograph type:** | Stone-Faiveley |
| **Rectifier type:** | Germanium |
| **Nominal supply voltage:** | 25kV ac |
| **Region of allocation:** | Midland |
| **Sector ownership:** | F, I, L, R |

Until 1986 the Class 85 fleet had a maximum speed of 100mph. It is understood that this will be returned to its former level in due course.

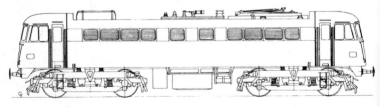

Above:
*This drawing is representative of the majority of this class. The window and ventilation arrangement on the opposite side of the body is different.*

Above:

*The Class 85 fleet, which is allocated to Crewe Electric depot, remains basically complete except for some locomotives that have received either fire or collision damage. Like the earlier ac types the same basic layout is followed, with windows being provided on one side and ventilation grilles on the other. The above illustration shows locomotive No 85039 from its No 1 end, while the lower plate shows No 85032 from the No 2 end. On the lower plate the main areas of equipment are marked. 1. Stone Faiveley pantograph, 2. Exhauster and compressor chokes, 3. Battery box, 4. Weak field resistors, 5. Traction motor cooling fan, 6. DC switchgear, 7. Transformer and cooling fans, 8. Dynamic brake equipment, 9. Rectifier and cooling fans, 10. Main air reservoirs.*
Both: John Tuffs

All InterCity 125 power cars are now painted in various InterCity livery schemes. Regrettably the same cannot be said for the coaching stock, with some 40% of the fleet still in BR blue. A full InterCity rake headed by No 43002 approaches Teignmouth on 20 April 1987 with the 09.25 Plymouth-Paddington.   Colin J. Marsden.

# Class 86

| | 86/1 | 86/2 | 86/4 |
|---|---|---|---|
| Sub-Class: | | | |
| Former Class codes: | AL6 | AL6 | AL6 |
| Number range: | 86101-86103 | 86204-86261 | 86401-86439 |
| Former number range: | [1] | [1] | [1] |
| Built by: | EE Ltd | EE Ltd & BR Doncaster | EE Ltd & BR Doncaster |
| Introduced: | As 86/1 1972[2] | As 86/2 1972-75[2] | As 86/4 1984/87[2] |
| Wheel arrangement: | Bo-Bo | Bo-Bo | Bo-Bo |
| Weight (operational): | 87 tonnes | 85 tonnes[3] | 83 tonnes[3] |
| Height (pantograph lowered): | 13ft 0in 9/16in (3.97m) | 13ft 0 9/16in (3.97m) | 13ft 0 9/16in (3.97m) |
| Width: | 8ft 8¼in (2.64m) | 8ft 8¼in (2.64m) | 8ft 8¼in (2.64m) |
| Length: | 58ft 6in (17.83m) | 58ft 6in (17.83m) | 58ft 6in (17.83m) |
| Minimum curve negotiable: | 6 chains (120.70m) | 6 chains (120.70m) | 6 chains (120.70m) |
| Maximum speed: | 110mph (177km/h) | 110mph (177km/h)[4] | 100mph (161km/h) |
| Wheelbase: | 43ft 6in (13.25m) | 43ft 6in (13.25m) | 43ft 6in (13.25m) |
| Bogie wheelbase: | 10ft 9in (3.27m) | 10ft 9in (3.27m) | 10ft 9in (3.27m) |
| Bogie pivot centres: | 32ft 9in (9.98m) | 32ft 9in (9.98m) | 32ft 9in (9.98m) |
| Wheel diameter: | 3ft 9¼in (1.15m) | 3ft 9½in (1.16m) | 3ft 9½in (1.16m) |
| Brake type: | Dual | Dual | Dual |
| Sanding equipment: | Pneumatic | Pneumatic | Pneumatic |
| Heating type: | Electric — Index 74 | Electric — Index 74 | Electric — Index 74 |
| Route availability: | 6 | 6 | 6 |
| Coupling restriction: | Not multiple fitted | TDM | [5] |
| Brake force: | 40 tonnes | 40 tonnes | 40 tonnes |
| Horsepower (continuous): | 5,000hp (3,730kW) | 4,040hp (3,014kW) | 4,040hp (3,014kW) |
| (maximum): | 7,860hp (5,860kW) | 6,100hp (4,550kW) | 5,900hp (4,400kW) |
| Tractive effort (maximum): | 58,000lb (258kN) | 46,500lb (207kN) | 58,000lb (258kN) |
| Number of traction motors: | 4 | 4 | 4 |
| Traction motor type: | GEC G412AZ | AEI 282BZ | AEI 282AZ |
| Control system: | HT Tap Changing | HT Tap Changing | HT Tap Changing |
| Gear ratio: | 32 : 73 | 22 : 65 | 22 : 65 |
| Pantograph type: | Brecknell Willis | Brecknell Willis/AEI | Stone-Faiveley/AEI |
| Rectifier type: | Silicon semi-conductor | Silicon semi-conductor | Silicon semi-conductor |

| **Nominal supply voltage:** | 25kV ac | 25kV ac | 25kV ac |
| **Region of allocation:** | Midland | Midland[6] | Midland[6] |
| **Sector ownership:** | I | I, N, R | F, I, L, N, R |

*Notes:*

[1] The Class 86 original numbers were E3101-E3200, renumbering was carried out at random, as modification work was effected.

[2] The Class 86s were originally introduced in 1965-66.

[3] A number of Class 86/2s and 86/4s have ballast weights which increase their weight by 1 tonne.

[4] Class 86/2s that have AEI pantographs are still restricted to 100mph running, while those fitted with the modern Brecknell Willis type, are permitted to operate at 110mph.

[5] Class 86/4s are fitted with multiple operation equipment, multiple operating is restricted to Class 86/4s, and Class 87/1s, as well as TDM equipment.

[6] All Class 86s are allocated to the LMR, but a number are diagrammed to work on the ER (GE) section.

## Subclass variations

Class 86/1: Locomotives fitted with revised electrical equipment and bogies as fitted to Class 87s.

Class 86/2: Locomotives fitted with flexicoil suspension, SAB wheels and AEI 282BZ traction motors.

Class 86/4: Locomotives fitted with flexicoil suspension, SAB wheels, multiple control equipment and AEI 282AZ traction motors.

A new Class 86/5 is now being introduced for the Freightliner sub-sector with a maximum speed of 75mph.

NO 2 END

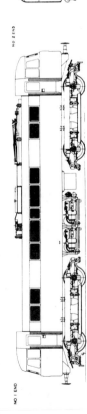

NO 1 END

*Above:*
*This drawing represents most members of the Class 86 fleet, although all locomotives are now fitted with Flexicoil suspension.*

Below:

The Class 86 fleet is divided into three sub-classes: 86/1, 86/2, and 86/4. The Class 86/1 fleet consists of three locomotives (Nos 86101-103) which were introduced in 1972 to evaluate equipment to be installed in the then proposed Class 87/0 locomotives. Although classified as Class 86s, these locomotives are technically Class 87/0s, having their bogie style and traction characteristics. The three machines are distinguishable from the remainder of the fleet by their BP9 bogies and modified roof equipment. All three Class 86/1s are allocated to Willesden depot and operated by the InterCity sector. No 86103 is illustrated. Colin J. Marsden

Above:

*Class 86 cab layout: 1. Train brake valve, 2. Locomotive brake valve, 3. Main reservoir gauge, 4. Brake cylinder gauge, 5. Vacuum gauge, 6. Brake pipe gauge, 7. Speedometer, 8. No 1 & 2 traction motor ampmeter, 9. No 3 & 4 traction motor ampmeter, 10. Notch indicator, 11. Notch indicator, 12. Line indicator, 13. Fault indicator, 14. ETS 'on' indicator, 15. Instrument light switch, 16. Tail light switch, 17. Marker light switch, 18. Foot warmer switch, 19. Cab heat switch, 20. Cab pre-heat switch, 21. Cab light switch, 22. Anti-slip brake button, 23. Windscreen washer button, 24. Windscreen wiper control, 25. Horn valve, 26. Pantograph 'up' button, 27. Pantograph 'down' button, 28. Headlight switch, 29. ETS 'on' button, 30. ETS 'off' button, 31. Power controller, 32. Master switch release button, 33. Master switch, 34. Master switch key socket, 35. Brake overcharge button.   Colin J. Marsden*

Below:

*The largest sub-class of the Class 86 fleet is Class 86/2 comprising 57 locomotives. The external arrangement of the locomotive differs on both sides, with one side having four grille panels and two windows and the other having nine grilles. No 86226 is illustrated from the window or corridor side, with the main equipment areas marked. 1. Flexicoil suspension, 2. Automatic power control equipment, 3. Brake cylinder, 4. Battery box, 5. Vacuum exhausters, 6. Main power/traction equipment, 7. Main transformer, 8. Brake equipment. All Class 86/2s are allocated to Willesden and operate both on WCML services, and those on the ER (GE) to Norwich.   Colin J. Marsden*

*Class 86 front end layout, applicable to all Class 86 sub-classes: 1. Marker lights, 2. Red 'tail' lights, 3. ETS jumper socket, 4. ETS jumper cable, 5. Vacuum pipe, 6. Coupling, 7. Brake pipe, 8. Main reservoir pipe, 9. Sand filler port. On some locomotives headlights are fitted either directly under the former route indicator box, or just above the ETS jumper box. All Class 86 locomotives will be fitted with TDM control cables in the near future (see page 135).* Colin J. Marsden

Below:

*The most recent addition to the Class 86 fleet is the Class 86/4 sub-section of which 38 are in traffic. These locomotives have flexicoil suspension and resilient wheelsets, and are fitted for multiple operation. Internally the locomotives are the same as the Class 86/2s. The fitting of multiple control jumpers gives an immediate recognition factor for this sub-class, and provides the facility for up to three locomotives to be operated by one driver. The multiple system is only compatible with other similar class members and Class 87/0 locomotives. No 86427 is illustrated from its No 2 end. Colin J. Marsden*

Bottom:

*The ownership of the Class 86s is shared between the InterCity, Parcels, Network SouthEast and Freight sectors. All examples carry either blue or InterCity livery, apart from No 86401 which is painted in Network SouthEast colours. No 86401 is illustrated at Liverpool Street. Note the headlight fitment. Brian Morrison*

Above:
*To enable 110mph operation, some Class 86/2s are fitted with Brecknell, Willis high speed pantographs, similar to those fitted to the Class 87/0s. Brecknell Willis-fitted No 86225 is illustrated at Greenholme on the climb to Shap summit.   Colin J. Marsden*

Below:
*Many Class 86 locomotives are now being fitted with a Time Division Multiplex (TDM) control system, enabling locomotives to be operated at the rear of trains when a suitable driving vehicle is provided. To connect this system between locomotive and train TDM jumpers are provided, shown here on the front of No 86426. These connections also provide for driver-guard communication.   Brian Morrison*

# Class 87

| Sub-Class: | 87/0 | 87/1 |
|---|---|---|
| Number range: | 87001-87035 | 87101 |
| Built by: | BREL Crewe | BREL Crewe |
| Introduced: | 1973-74 | 1977 |
| Wheel arrangement: | Bo-Bo | Bo-Bo |
| Weight (operational): | 83 tonnes | 79 tonnes |
| Height (pantograph lowered): | 13ft 1¼in (3.99m) | 13ft 1¼in (3.99m) |
| Width: | 8ft 8¼in (2.64m) | 8ft 8¼in (2.64m) |
| Length: | 58ft 6in (17.83m) | 58ft 6in (17.83m) |
| Minimum curve negotiable: | 6 chains (120.70m) | 6 chains (120.70m) |
| Maximum speed: | 110mph (177km/h) | 110mph (177km/h) |
| Wheelbase: | 43ft 6⅛in (13.25m) | 43ft 6⅛in (13.25m) |
| Bogie wheelbase: | 10ft 9in (3.27m) | 10ft 9in (3.27m) |
| Bogie pivot centres: | 32ft 9in (9.98m) | 32ft 9in (9.98m) |
| Wheel diameter: | 3ft 9½in (1.16m) | 3ft 9½in (1.16m) |
| Brake type: | Air | Air |
| Sanding equipment: | Pneumatic | Pneumatic |
| Heating type: | Electric — Index 95 | Electric — Index 95 |
| Route availability: | 6 | 6 |
| Coupling restriction: | Within type and Class 86 | Within type and Class 86[1] |
| Brake force: | 40 tonnes | 40 tonnes |
| Horsepower (continuous): | 5,000hp (3,730kW) | 4,850hp (3,620kW) |
| (maximum): | 7,860hp (5,860kW) | 7,250hp (5,401kW) |
| Tractive effort (maximum): | 58,000lb (258kN) | 58,000lb (258kN) |
| Number of traction motors: | 4 | 4 |
| Traction motor type: | GEC G412AZ | GEC G412BZ |
| Control system: | HT Tap Changing | Thyristor |
| Gear ratio: | 32 : 73 | 32 : 73 |
| Pantograph type: | Brecknell Willis HS | Brecknell Willis HS |
| Nominal supply voltage: | 25kV ac | 25kV ac |
| Region of allocation: | Midland | Midland |
| Sector ownership: | I, L | F |

[1] Also fitted with TDM equipment.

## Subclass variations

Class 87/0 — Basic locomotive.
Class 87/1 — Class 87 fitted with thyristor control equipment in place of HT tap changing system.

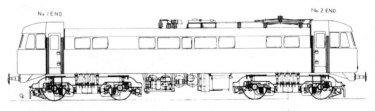

Above:
*This drawing is representative of the majority of the class. Window and ventilation arrangements differ on either side of the body. Class 87/0 are fitted with Brecknell, Willis pantographs.*

**Above:**
*Class 87 cab layout: 1. Train brake valve, 2. Locomotive brake valve, 3. Anti-slip brake button, 4. Windscreen wash/wipe control, 5. Warning horn valve, 6. Brake overcharge plunger, 7. AWS reset button, 8. Headlight switch, 9. Pantograph up button, 10. Pantograph down button, 11. ETS 'on' button, 12. ETS 'off' button, 13. Master switch (FOR/NET/REV), 14. Master switch release button, 15. Master switch key socket, 16. Power controller, 17. AWS indicator, 18. Main reservoir gauge, 19. Brake cylinder gauge, 20. Brake pipe gauge, 21. Speedometer, 22. No 1 & 2 traction motor ammeter, 23. No 3 & 4 traction motor ammeter, 24. Notch indicator, 25. Notch indicator, 26. Line indicator, 27. Fault light, 28. ETS 'on' light, 29. Instrument light switch, 30. Tail light switch, 31. Marker light switch, 32. Foot warmer switch, 33. Cab heat switch, 34. Cab pre-heat switch, 35. Cab light switch, 36. Marker light switch, 37. Demister switch, 38. Parking brake indicator, 39. Parking brake switch, 40. Cab ventilation.*
GEC Traction Ltd

**Below:**
*Two sub-classes of Class 87 are currently in service, the original type (now Class 87/0) being introduced in 1973-74 for the new 'Electric Scot' services. The locomotives follow the same basic design as the previous Class 86 except that the cab windscreens are divided into only two sections. The two sides of the locomotives are different, one having nine grille sections in the upper portion, and the other having four grilles and two windows. All locomotives are fitted with Brecknell, Willis high speed pantographs giving a top speed of 110mph. No 87012, the first locomotive in InterCity livery, is illustrated from its No 1 end. Note: When the InterCity livery was adopted a number of minor refinements were incorporated.* Colin J. Marsden

Below:

*Class 87 front end, fitted with TDM jumpers: 1. Multiple control jumper cable, 2. Multiple control jumper recepticle, 3. TDM jumper cable, 4. Red 'tail' light, 5. Marker light, 6. High intensity headlight, 7. Coupling, 8. Brake pipe, 9. Main reservoir pipe, 10. ETS jumper cable, 11. ETS jumper socket.   Colin J. Marsden*

**Above:**
*The final locomotive of the Class 87 build was classified 87/1, numbered 87101 and fitted with sophisticated 'chopper' control equipment as a test rig for the next generation of electric traction. After entering service the locomotive was subjected to stringent testing both under normal and chopper control systems. No 87101 looks exactly the same as a Class 87/0, and is allocated to Willesden.   Colin J. Marsden*

**Below:**
*To enable driver-guard communication and remote operation, the Class 87 fleet are fitted with TDM jumpers which connect with suitable cables on Mk 2 and Mk 3 stock. The TDM cables can be seen on the front of blue liveried No 87021 leading InterCity liveried No 87005 on a southbound steel train seen descending Shap in July 1986.*
*Colin J. Marsden*

Above and below:
When introduced, the Class 87s were painted in standard rail blue, but after the decision to introduce a new InterCity livery the Class 87 fleet were the first to benefit. Since its introduction a number of variations have occurred, mainly in the position of the dark

scheme as applied to No 87008 City of Liverpool. Note the revision of the nameplate position on InterCity-liveried locomotives. In February 1987 a further livery revision was made when the dark grey area was replaced by dark brown. The first locomotive modified was No 86228.  Both: Colin J. Marsden

# Class 89

| | |
|---|---|
| **Number:** | 89001 |
| **Built by:** | BREL Crewe, Brush Ltd |
| **Introduced:** | 1987 |
| **Wheel arrangement:** | Co-Co |
| **Weight (operational):** | 105 tonnes |
| **Height (pantograph lowered):** | 13ft 0½in (3.97m) |
| **Width:** | 8ft 11½in (2.73m) |
| **Length:** | 64ft 11in (19.79m) |
| **Minimum curve negotiable:** | |
| **Maximum speed:** | 125mph (201km/h) |
| **Wheelbase:** | 49ft 6½in (15.10m) |
| **Bogie wheelbase:** | 14ft 5in (4.39m) |
| **Bogie pivot centres:** | 35ft 8¼in (10.87m) |
| **Wheel diameter:** | 3ft 9½in (1.15m) |
| **Brake type:** | Air (Rheostatic) |
| **Sanding equipment:** | Not fitted |
| **Heating type:** | Electric — Index 95 |
| **Route availability:** | 6 |
| **Coupling restriction:** | Not multiple fitted |
| **Brake force:** | |
| **Horsepower (continuous):** | 5,830hp (4,350kW) |
| **(maximum):** | |
| **Tractive effort (maximum):** | 46,200lb (205kN) |
| **Traction motor type:** | Brush |
| **Control system:** | Thyristor |
| **Gear ratio:** | |
| **Pantograph type:** | Brecknell Willis HS |
| **Nominal supply voltage:** | 25kV ac |
| **Region of allocation:** | |
| **Sector ownership:** | |

Right:

*The Class 89 commenced trial running on the WCML between Crewe and London during May 1987, usually hauling part of the experimental International train, together with two of the Derby test cars. On some trips the maximum permitted speed was 135mph. On 7 May 1987 No 89001 passes Madeley with a Willesden-Crewe return special.* J. Winkle

Above:

*Cab layout of Class 89, 1. Parking brake 'off' button, 2. Parking brake indicator, 3. Parking brake 'on' button, 4. Brake overcharge button, 5. Brake full bore button, 6. LED test button, 7. De-mister switch, 8. Cab heat control, 9. Body light switch, 10, Tail light switch, 11. Marker light switch, 12. Clip board light switch, 13. Cab light switch, 14. Desk light switch, 15. Desk light switch, 16. Brake controller, 17. Emergency brake plunger, 18. Main reservoir pressure gauge, 19. Bogie brake cylinder gauge, 20. Brake pipe pressure gauge, 21. AWS alarm, 22. AWS indicator, 23. TM Amps, 24. Speedometer, 25. Headlight failed indicator, 26. Wheelslip indicator, 27. AWS isolated indicator, 28. Passenger communication alarm indicator, 29. Rheostatic brake failed indicator, 30. General fault indicator, 31. Parking brake 'on' indicator, 32. Traction over temperature light, 33. Line 'on' indicator, 34. Fire bottle isolated indicator, 35. ETS 'on' indicator, 36. ETS 'on' button, 37. ETS 'off' button, 38. Pantograph 'up' button, 39. Pantograph 'down' button, 40. Guard's intercom button, 41. Fire alarm button, 42. Automatic speed selector switch, 43. Headlight switch, 44. Windscreen wiper control, 45. Master switch, 46. AWS re-set button, 47. Horn switch, 48. Power controller, 49. Telephone.   Michael J. Collins*

# Class 90

| | |
|---|---|
| **Number range:** | 90001-900xx |
| **Built by:** | BREL Crewe |
| **Introduced:** | 1987-89 |
| **Wheel arrangement:** | Bo-Bo |
| **Weight (operational):** | 82½ tonnes |
| **Height (pantograph lowered):** | |
| **Width:** | |
| **Length:** | 61ft 6in (18.74m) |
| **Minimum curve negotiable:** | 4 chains (80.80m) |
| **Maximum speed:** | 110mph (177km/h) |
| **Wheelbase:** | 43ft 6in (13.26m) |
| **Bogie wheelbase:** | 10ft 9in (3.28m) |
| **Bogie pivot centres:** | 32ft 9in |
| **Wheel diameter:** | 3ft 9½in (1.16m) |
| **Brake type:** | Air (Rheostatic) |
| **Sanding equipment:** | Pneumatic |
| **Heating type:** | Electric — Index 95 |
| **Route availability:** | 7 |
| **Coupling restriction:** | Fitted with TDM |
| **Brake force:** | 40 tonnes |
| **Horsepower (continuous):** | 4,850hp (3,620kW) |
| **(maximum):** | 7,250hp (5,401kW) |
| **Tractive effort (maximum):** | |
| **Number of traction motors:** | 4 |
| **Traction motor type:** | GEC |
| **Control system:** | Thyristor |
| **Gear ratio:** | |
| **Pantograph type:** | Brecknell Willis HS |
| **Nominal supply voltage:** | 25kV ac |
| **Region of allocation:** | Midland |
| **Sector ownership:** | I |

Cab details are identical to Class 91 and is illustrated on p147.

Below:
*Class 90, No 90003, is seen at Preston on a crew familiarisation run.* Peter Hill

Above:
*Originally to be classified as Class 872, the new third generation of 25kV ac electric locomotive eventually emerged in 1987 as Class 90. This fleet of 50 locomotives are immediately recognisable from earlier ac types by the steeply-raked front end and revised bodyside styling. This illustration shows No 90001 from the main equipment (five grille) side, from the No 1 end.   Colin J. Marsden*

Below:
*General arrangement view of Class 90 showing the battery box side with only two grille panels in the upper bodyside. The livery applied to the Class 90 is standard InterCity with small numbers below each cabside window at waist height.   Brian Morrison*

# Class 91

| | |
|---|---|
| **Number:** | 91001-91050 |
| **Built by:** | BREL Crewe by GEC |
| **Introduced:** | 1988-90 |
| **Wheel arrangement:** | Bo-Bo |
| **Weight (operational):** | 80 tonnes |
| **Height (pantograph lowered):** | 12ft 4in (3.75m) |
| **Width:** | 9ft 0in (2.74m) |
| **Length:** | 63ft 8in (19.40m) |
| **Minimum curve negotiable:** | 4 chains (80.80m) |
| **Maximum speed:** | 140mph (225km/h) |
| **Wheelbase:** | 56ft 5½in (17.20m) |
| **Bogie wheelbase:** | 10ft 11⅞in (3.35m) |
| **Bogie pivot centres:** | 34ft 5½in (10.50m) |
| **Wheel diameter:** | 3ft 3½in (1.00m) |
| **Brake type:** | Air (Rheostatic) |
| **Sanding equipment:** | Pneumatic |
| **Heating type:** | Electric — Index |
| **Route availability:** | |
| **Coupling restriction:** | Fitted with TDM |
| **Brake force:** | |
| **Horsepower (continuous):** | 6,080hp (4,530kW) |
| **(maximum):** | 6,310hp (4,700kW) |
| **Tractive effort (maximum):** | |
| **Traction motor type:** | GEC |
| **Control system:** | Thyristor |
| **Gear ratio:** | |
| **Pantograph type:** | Brecknell Willis HS |
| **Nominal supply voltage:** | 25kV ac |
| **Region of allocation:** | Eastern |
| **Sector ownership:** | |

Above right:

*Class 91 cab layout: 1. Park-brake 'on' button, 2. Park-brake indicator, 3. Park-brake 'off' button, 4. Brake overcharge switch, 5. Instrument light switch, 6. Cab light switch, 7. Clip board light switch, 8. Cab air treatment switch, heat/vent/cool, 9. Cab air treatment switch, high/low, 10. Sand button, 11. Foot warmer switch, 12. De-mister switch, 13. Tail light switch, 14. Marker light switch, 15. Emergency brake plunger, 16. Brake controller, 17. Bogie brake cylinder gauge, 18. Clock, 19. Main reservoir gauge, 20. AWS alarm, 21. AWS indicator, 22. Brake pipe gauge, 23. AWS isolate warning light, 24. Headlight warning light, 25. Wheelslip warning light, 26. General fault light, 27. Tilt warning light, 28. Electric train supply (ETS) warning light, 29. Line indicator, 30. Pantograph auto-drop light, 31. High-speed brake indicator light, 32. Pre-set speed control, 33. Thermo display, 34. Speedometer, 35. Noticeboard, 36. Driver/guard call button, 37. ETS 'on' button, 38. Passenger communication override button, 39. Pantograph up or reset button, 40. Fire alarm test button, 41. ETS 'off' button, 42. Fire extinguisher delay button, 43. Pantograph down button, 44. Locomotive/shore radio system, 45. Headlight switch, 46. Tractive effort boost button, 47. ashtray, 48. Power controller, 49. windscreen wiper controller, 50. Master switch key socket, 51. Master switch, 52. AWS reset button, 53. Horn valve. Cab illustrated is from slab end of No 91001.   Colin J. Marsden*

Right:

*A major change in locomotive styling emerged in February 1988 when the first Class 91 was unveiled. The drawgear arrangements are standard with buckeye couplers being provided. TDM jumpers are also provided stowed behind two lockable panels on the body ends (above the light clusters). The illustration shows the locomotive from the slab No 2 end.   Both: Colin J. Marsden*

# Class 43 (IC125 Power Cars)

| | |
|---|---|
| **Set classification:** | 253, 254 |
| **Number range:** | 43002-43198 |
| **Built by:** | BREL Crewe |
| **Introduced:** | 1976-82 |
| **Wheel arrangement:** | Bo-Bo |
| **Weight (operational):** | 70 tonnes |
| **Height:** | 12ft 9in (3.88m) |
| **Width:** | 8ft 11in (2.71m) |
| **Length:** | 58ft 5in (17.80m) |
| **Minimum curve negotiable:** | 4 chains (80.46m) |
| **Maximum speed:** | 125mph (201km/h) |
| **Wheelbase:** | 42ft 3in (12.87m) |
| **Bogie wheelbase:** | 8ft 6in (2.59m) |
| **Bogie pivot centres:** | 33ft 9in (10.28m) |
| **Wheel diameter (driving):** | 3ft 4in (1.01m) |
| **Brake type:** | Air |
| **Sanding equipment:** | Not fitted |
| **Heating type:** | Electric |
| **Route availability:** | 6 |
| **Multiple coupling restriction:** | Not fitted |
| **Brake force:** | |
| **Engine type (43002-166/171-198):** | Paxman Valenta 12PR200L |
| **(43167-170):** | Mirrlees Blackstone MB190 |
| **Horsepower (43002-166/171-198):** | 2,250hp (1,676kW) |
| **(43167-170):** | 2,400hp (1,788kW) |
| **Power at rail (43002-166/171-198):** | 1,770hp (1,320kW) |
| **(43167-170):** | |
| **Tractive effort:** | 17,980lb (80kN) |
| **Cylinder bore (43002-166/171-198):** | |
| **(43167-171):** | |
| **Cylinder stroke (43002-166/171-198):** | |
| **(43167-170):** | |
| **Main alternator type:** | Brush BA1001B |
| **Number of traction motors:** | 4 |
| **Traction motor type (43002-123/153-198):** | Brush TMH68-46 |
| **(43124-152):** | GEC G417AZ |
| **Gear ratio:** | |
| **Fuel tank capacity:** | 1,000gal (4,546lit) |
| **Cooling water capacity:** | |
| **Lubricating oil capacity:** | |
| **Regions of allocation:** | Eastern, Western, Scottish |
| **Sector ownership:** | I |

Cars Nos 43002-43152 were built with full guards' facilities, and classified DMB, cars
Nos 43153-198 were built without this facility and classified DM. DMB cars have an
additional window to the rear of the luggage door.

*Note:*
The IC125 power cars, which are numerically classified as 43, are more usually identified
by their set classifications of 253 or 254. However, as they basically function as
locomotives they are included in this volume.

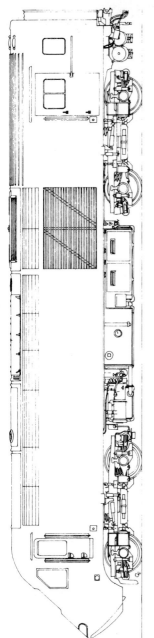

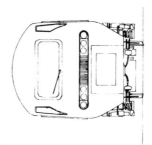

Above:
Two types of IC125 power car are in existence — DM (Driving Motor) and DMB (Driving Motor Brake). This drawing is of a DMB in the number range 43003-43152. Both sides of the car are identical. On DM cars, the window to the rear of the guard's door is omitted.

Below:
In May 1987 a new livery was launched for the High Speed Train fleet, which has dispensed with the 125 logo, and adopted the legend 'INTERCITY' in a bold face together with a silver swallow motif.
Brian Morrison

Below:

*Unlike conventional locomotives the Class 43 power cars only have driving facilities at one end, the other end of the vehicle originally containing guard's accommodation which is now being progressively removed. The upper plate shows a power car from the nose end, while the lower plate is taken from the guards or luggage end. Main equipment areas are indicated: 1. No 1 bogie, 2. No 2 bogie, 3. Air compressor, 4. Fuel tank, 5. Battery box, 6. Fire pull handle, 7. Electronic control equipment & No 1 traction motor blower, 8. Power unit and alternator compartment, 9. Radiator compartment, 10. No 2 Traction motor blower and emergency coupling box, 11. Guard's van and office (now being removed), 12. Air reservoirs.   Both: Colin J. Marsden*

Above:
InterCity 125 cab layout: 1. ETS dimmer switch, 2. De-icer/mister switch, 3. Desk light switch, 4. Tail light switch, 5. Tail light switch, 6. Marker light switch, 7. Headlight switch, 8. Engine room light switch, 9. Cab light switch, 10. Brake controller, 11. Power controller, 12. AWS reset button, 13. Horn switch, 14. Master switch, 15. AWS indicator, 16. Inspection light socket, 17. Brake test switch, 18. Windscreen wiper valve, 19. Air conditioning switch, 20. ETS 'on' button, 21. Parking brake indicator, 22. Parking brake 'on' button, 23. Fire alarm test button, 24. ETS 'off' button, 25. Train supply indicator, 26. Parking brake 'off' button, 27. Brake overcharge button (not used), 28. Main reservoir gauge, 29. Brake cylinder gauge, 30. Brake pipe gauge, 31. AWS in/out indicator, 32. Fault indicator, 33. AWS/DSD alarm, 34. Start signal and telephone call alarm, 35. Speedometer, 36. Ampmeter, 37. Clock, 38. Telephone, 39. Wheelslip indicator, 40. Engine stopped indicator, 41. Engine start button, 42. Engine stop button, 43. Buzzer to guard.   Colin J. Marsden

Below:
To provide remote driving trailer vehicles for TDM-fitted electric locomotives, and to enable Class 91 testing to commence on the ECML, a fleet of four IC125 power cars have been converted into Driving Van Trailers (DVTs). The conversion has rendered the vehicles powerless, and called for the fitting of conventional drawgear and ETS jumpers. The first converted car, No 43014, is illustrated.   Michael J. Collins

# Class 98

| | 7 | 8 | 9 |
|---|---|---|---|
| Number: | 7 | 8 | 9 |
| Built by: | GWR Swindon | GWR Swindon | GWR Swindon* |
| Introduced: | 1923 | 1923 | 1924 |
| Type: | 2-6-2T | 2-6-2T | 2-6-2T |
| Gauge: | 1ft 11½in (0.59m) | 1ft 11½in (0.59m) | 1ft 11½in (0.59m) |
| Weight (operational): | 25 tonnes | 25 tonnes | 22 tonnes |
| Height: | 9ft 0in (2.74m) | 9ft 0in (2.74m) | 9ft 0in (2.74m) |
| Width: | 8ft 0in (2.43m) | 8ft 0in (2.43m) | 6ft 0in (1.82m) |
| Length: | 21ft 10in (6.65m) | 21ft 10in (6.65m) | 21ft 10in (6.65m) |
| Tractive effort: | 10,510lb (67kN) | 10,510lb (67kN) | 10,510lb (67kN) |
| Wheelbase (coupled): | 6ft 0in (1.82m) | 6ft 0in (1.82m) | 6ft 0in (1.82m) |
| Wheelbase (total): | 16ft 10in (5.13m) | 16ft 10in (5.13m) | 16ft 10in (5.13m) |
| Coupled wheel dia: | 2ft 6in (0.76m) | 2ft 6in (0.76m) | 2ft 6in (0.76m) |
| Pony wheel diameter: | 2ft 0in (0.60m) | 2ft 0in (0.60m) | 2ft 0in (0.60m) |
| Brake type: | Vacuum | Vacuum | Vacuum |
| Boiler pressure: | 165lb/sq in | 165lb/sq in | 150lb/sq in |
| Coal capacity: | 32cu ft | 32cu ft | 32cu ft |
| Water capacity: | 520gal (2,364lit) | 520gal (2,364lit) | 650gal (2,955lit) |
| Cylinder bore: | 11½in (0.29m) | 11½in (0.29m) | 11in (0.27m) |
| Cylinder stroke: | 17in (0.43m) | 17in (0.43m) | 17in (0.43m) |
| Allocation: | Vale of Rheidol | Vale of Rheidol | Vale of Rheidol |

| | 10 |
|---|---|
| Number: | 10 |
| Built by: | Brecon Mountain Rly |
| Introduced: | 1988 |
| Type: | 0-6-0 |
| Gauge: | 1ft 11½in (0.59m) |
| Weight: | 12¾ tonnes |
| Length: | |
| Height: | |
| Width: | |
| Wheelbase: | |
| Wheel diameter: | |
| Brake type: | Vacuum |
| Engine type: | Caterpillar 3304T |
| Engine horsepower: | 140hp |
| Power at rail: | |
| Tractive effort: | |
| Cylinder bore: | |
| Cylinder stroke: | |
| Transmission: | Mechanical twin-disk |
| Fuel capacity: | |
| Cooling water capacity: | |
| Lub oil capacity: | |
| Allocation: | Vale of Rheidol |

*Nominally a rebuild of a Davies & Metcalfe 1902 product but actually built new at Swindon in 1924.

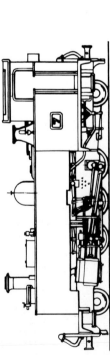

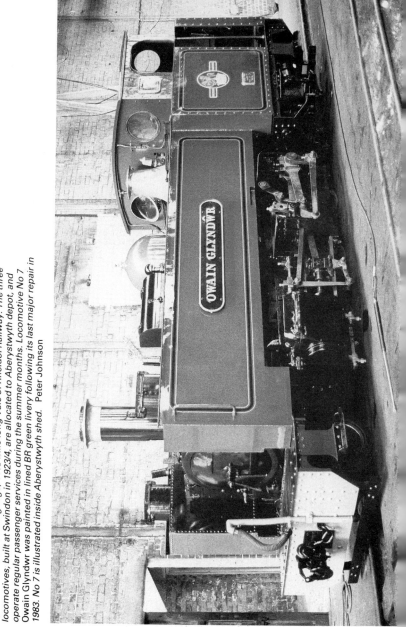

The only steam traction operated by BR consists of three 2-6-2T locomotives, which operate on the 1ft 11½in gauge, 11½-mile long Vale of Rheidol Railway. The three locomotives, built at Swindon in 1923/4, are allocated to Aberystwyth depot, and operate regular passenger services during the summer months. Locomotive No 7 Owain Glyndwr was painted in lined BR green livery following its last major repair in 1983. No 7 is illustrated inside Aberystwyth shed.    Peter Johnson

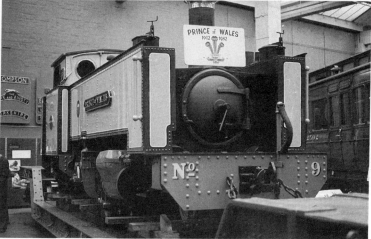

Top left:
*Locomotives Nos 7 and 8 were constructed by the GWR at Swindon in 1923, while No 9 was built in 1924, although records show the locomotive as being a rebuild of a 1902 Davis & Metcalfe product. At various times the Vale of Rheidol locomotives have carried different liveries, mainly authentic, but with some local customisation. No 8, which for many years was named* Llewellyn, *was repainted into Cambrian black livery in spring 1987. In this scheme the locomotive has lost its name, but bears the Cambrian legend on the side.* Peter Johnson

Left:
*No 7* Owain Glyndwr, *in lined BR green livery, approaches Devil's Bridge with a train from Aberystwyth on 21 July 1984.* John Chalcraft

Above:
*Since 1982, Vale of Rheidol No 9* Prince of Wales *has carried yellow ochre livery, which looks extremely smart on this comparatively small locomotive. No 9 holds the distinction of being the oldest BR-operated locomotive still in use today, and, judging by its condition will continue to be in traffic for many years to come. In the upper plate No 9 approaches Nanyronen, while the lower plate shows the locomotive on display at the NRM York. Note that the locomotive is mounted on a well wagon.* Both: Peter Johnson

# Departmental Locomotives Class 97

| Depart. No | Former number | Name | Use | Location |
|---|---|---|---|---|
| 97204 | 31326 | — | Test Train locomotive | Derby RTC |
| 97251 | 25305 | — | Electric Train Supply locomotive | Carlisle |
| 97252 | 25314 | — | Electric Train Supply locomotive | Old Oak Common |
| 97403 | 46035 | Ixion | Test Train locomotive | Derby RTC |
| 97404 | 46045 | — | Spares locomotive for 97403 (stored) | Derby RTC |
| 97409 | 45022 | — | Departmental Traction | Tinsley |
| 97410 | 45029 | — | Departmental Traction | Tinsley |
| 97411 | 45034 | — | Departmental Traction | Tinsley |
| 97412 | 45040 | — | Departmental Traction | Tinsley |
| 97413 | 45066 | — | Departmental Traction | Tinsley |
| 97651 | PWM651 | — | Civil Engineer's locomotive | Cardiff |
| 97653 | PWM653 | — | Civil Engineer's locomotive | Cardiff |
| 97654 | PWM654 | — | Civil Engineer's locomotive | Reading |
| 97701 | M61136 | — | M&EE Battery locomotive | Birkenhead |
| 97702 | M61139 | — | M&EE Battery locomotive | Birkenhead |
| 97703 | M61182 | — | M&EE Battery locomotive | Cricklewood |
| 97704 | M61185 | — | M&EE Battery locomotive | Cricklewood |
| 97705 | M61184 | — | M&EE Battery locomotive | Cricklewood |
| 97706 | M61189 | — | M&EE Battery locomotive | Cricklewood |
| 97707 | M61166 | — | M&EE Battery locomotive | Hornsey |
| 97708 | M61173 | — | M&EE Battery locomotive | Hornsey (stored) |
| 97709 | M61172 | — | M&EE Battery locomotive | Hornsey (stored) |
| 97710 | M61175 | — | M&EE Battery locomotive | Slade Green |
| 97800 | 08600 | Ivor | M&EE Shunting locomotive | Ryde |
| 97805 | 03079 | — | Civil Engineers locomotive | Cardiff |
| 97806 | 09017 | — | Severn Tunnel Emergency locomotive | Marylebone |
| ADB968000 | D8243 | — | Electric Train Supply locomotive | Crewe |
| ADB968021 | 84009 | — | M&EE Mobile Load Bank locomotive | Toton |
| ADB968024 | 45017 | — | M&EE Training locomotive | Eastfield |
| ADB968025 | 27207 | — | M&EE Training locomotive | Toton |
| ADB968026 | 25908 | — | M&EE Training locomotive | Eastfield |
| ADB968027 | 25912 | — | M&EE Training locomotive | Holbeck |
| ADB968028 | 27224 | — | M&EE Training locomotive | Eastfield |

Class 31 No 31326 under the Departmental banner as No 97204. The locomotive is painted in the Division's grey and red livery with a black and white waistband. The locomotive is seen arriving at the Railway Technical Centre in February 1988, after its first main line run. Colin J. Marsden

Top:
*In 1983, three redundant Class 25 locomotives were rebuilt at Aberdeen into non-powered ETS locomotives, primarily for use in Scotland where steam heat fitted locomotives were rostered to haul ETS-fitted stock. Since the vehicles were made redundant in Scotland they have found use south of the Border. Nos 97250/1 are painted in blue and grey livery, while No 97252 sports full InterCity livery and is now used to provide ETS on steam specials operating from Marylebone. No 97252 is illustrated at Derby. Note the ETS socket and jumper on the front end.   John Tuffs*

Above:
*Another locomotive taken over by the Research Division at Derby is Class 46 No 46035. Now renumbered 97403 and named Ixion, the locomotive is operated by the vehicle dynamics section for adhesion tests. Several external modifications have been carried out since its days in general traffic, including the installation of nose-end jumpers, and external panels for holding cables. No 97403 is painted in departmental blue and red livery.   Colin J. Marsden*

Above:

*Class 97/7 is used for a fleet of five two-vehicle locomotive sets used by the M&EE department for tunnel section maintenance operations. The locomotive pairs were rebuilt between 1974/80 from redundant Class 501 electric multiple unit cars. Each pair is formed of two individually numbered vehicles, their allocation being to Birkenhead and Hornsey. All are painted in conventional rail blue except Nos 97707/08 which were repainted in early 1987 in Network SouthEast livery. The NSE liveried pair are illustrated. Front end equipment consists of power jumpers, coupling, air and main reservoir connections, headlights, and tail lights. These locomotives are usually powered by battery packs, stored in the former seating bays.   Colin J. Marsden*

Below:

*The SR depot and regional workshops at Slade Green near Dartford operates a former Class 08 under the departmental flag. Numbered 97800 and named Ivor, the locomotive is painted in Network SouthEast livery and is used for depot pilot work. For full technical details reference should be made to the Class 08/0 section. No 97800 is seen stabled at Slade Green.   Brian Morrison*

Below:
*When withdrawn from capital stock Class 45/0 No 45017 was taken into departmental stock at Toton depot as a non-active M&EE maintenance training vehicle. The locomotive retained its blue livery, the only external alteration being the addition of its departmental No ADB968024. The locomotive is illustrated at Toton depot in May 1987.*
Colin J. Marsden

## Railfreight sub-Sector symbols

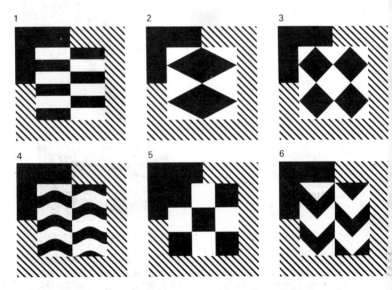

1 *General Railfreight.*
2 *Speedlink Distribution.*
3 *Railfreight Coal.*
4 *Railfreight Petroleum.*
5 *Railfreight Construction.*
6 *Railfreight Metals & Automotives.*